WORLD HISTORY
IN MINUTES

TAT WOOD & DOROTHY AIL

WORLD HISTORY IN MINUTES

TAT WOOD & DOROTHY AIL

Quercus

CONTENTS

THE RENAISSANCE

THE AGE OF REVOLUTIONS

THE AGE OF EMPIRES

THE 20TH CENTURY
AND BEYOND

Introduction

In selecting 200 short pieces to represent everything people have done we had to impose strict criteria. Did this incident, trend, nation, or person have a knock—on effect? Is it what a casual reader, picking up a book like this, wants to find out about in a hurry? Anything in this book is either something that has passed into public consciousness (maybe without most people knowing why—was Ivan IV of Russia really so terrible?) or is there to explain how we got from there to here.

We argued across the Atlantic about what should go in and why. Most of these pieces are encounters between one culture and another. For most of history those encounters are either military or commercial—or both—but some are about how ideas spread. We sought to punctuate terse accounts of massacres with more positive underlying trends.

Any one of these topics deserves a book-length discussion but this will get anyone interested started. We had to omit many pet subjects—Sabbatai Tsevi, the Lost City of Zimbabwe, the Franco-Prussian War, Prohibition, the invention of the novel. It becomes more Eurocentric as we come closer to today simply because the main story of the past five centuries involves Europeans at first treating other places as theirs, and later being asked to leave.

This book can only hope to offer a starting-point, although we hope it's comprehensive enough for everyday domestic use and will inspire further investigation elsewhere.

Tat Wood and Dorothy Ail

Lucy and her kin

One of the most famous fossils ever discovered, Lucy is the skeletal remains of an *Australopithecus afarensis*. Found in Ethiopia in 1974, she lived around 3.2 million years ago and was a bipedal hominid, with feet adapted for walking upright.

The history of human evolution extends both forward and backward from this point. Hominidae, the taxonomic family that humans share with their closest living relatives, the great apes (gorillas, chimpanzees, orangutans, and bonobos, the last controversially suggested to be closer to Lucy than modern humans) shared a common ancestry until quite recently in evolutionary terms, perhaps differentiating 6 million years or so ago. The first beings to walk upright comfortably seem to have been the *Australopithecus* genus, developing around 4 million years ago; they had smaller brains than even modern apes, and became extinct perhaps 2 million years ago. But they were able to develop tools, and genus *Homo* (which includes modern humans) evolved from them.

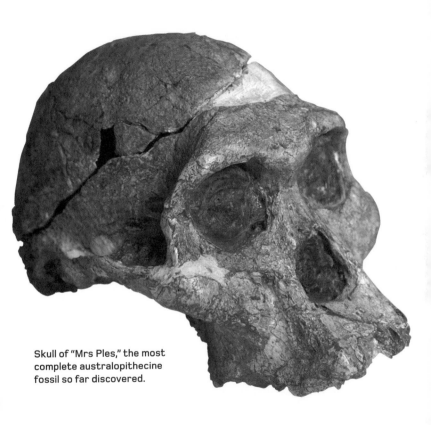

Skull of "Mrs Ples," the most complete australopithecine fossil so far discovered.

Tools, art, and belief

While many animals have learned to manipulate objects such as twigs to release food from inaccessible places, humans are the clearest example of what psychologists call "theory of mind." Early art indicates that this is as old as humanity—depictions of people and events are physical manifestations of mental processes, made to look recognizable to others, and with this came other significant abilities.

One is that an individual can imagine what another individual might do; verbal communication can go beyond information and orders into storytelling and attempts to guess another's reactions: associated regions of the brain developed rapidly in this period (some have suggested that civilization began with the ability to gossip). Another is that complex and abstract notions can be relayed, including plans for hunts, or future projects—things that cannot be seen. A third consequence is a realization that this ability ends when an individual dies: surprisingly early, we find humans buried with personal objects.

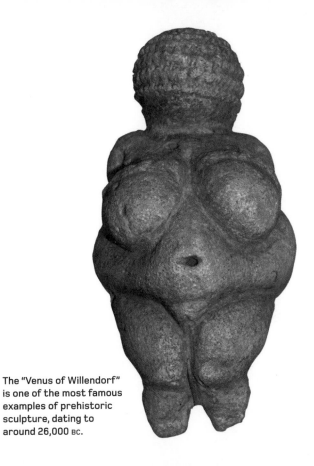

The "Venus of Willendorf" is one of the most famous examples of prehistoric sculpture, dating to around 26,000 BC.

Out of Africa

The genus *Homo* evolved in Africa a little less than 2.5 million years ago, characterized by increasingly large brains that equipped them better for survival—their predecessors the australopithecines became extinct soon thereafter. Mary and Louis Leakey became famous for their discovery of the *Homo habilis* site in Tanzania's Olduvai Gorge—a small apelike biped that was skilled with stone tools (hence the name). Later hominids were larger, stronger, and more anthropomorphic.

The fossil record shows that hominids spread from Africa to Europe and Asia in multiple waves beginning about 2 million years ago (exactly how many species were involved, and how recently some survived, remains uncertain). They appear to have developed vocalization, hunter-gatherer social groups, and the use of fire over the next million years. The current scientific consensus, supported by DNA studies, is that modern humans arose in Africa 200,000 years ago, before spreading out, replacing, and interbreeding with other hominids.

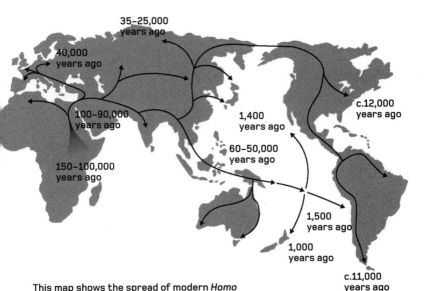

35–25,000
years ago

40,000
years ago

100–90,000
years ago

150–100,000
years ago

1,400
years ago

60–50,000
years ago

c.12,000
years ago

1,500
years ago

1,000
years ago

c.11,000
years ago

This map shows the spread of modern *Homo sapiens* out of Africa with approximate times of arrival—other hominid species had made similar journeys long before.

Neanderthals

Homo neanderthalensis's close affinity to modern humans and European stronghold meant that it was the first fossil hominid to attract attention (discovered in Germany's Neander valley in 1857). The Neanderthals seem to have settled after the first wave of hominid migration from Africa and to have persisted until about 40,000 years ago. *Homo sapiens*, meanwhile, may have arrived from Africa 60,000 years ago, so could have played a major role in Neanderthal extinction. DNA evidence for interbreeding is as yet inconclusive.

Scientists originally surmised that Neanderthals were unintelligent, hunchbacked beings, largely because one of the first skeletons found was of an arthritic man. More recent finds have shown that they were physically powerful, and evidence is increasing of abstract reasoning and large cerebral capacity. Physically capable of limited speech, they had sophisticated flint tools and religious rites—many burial sites have been found.

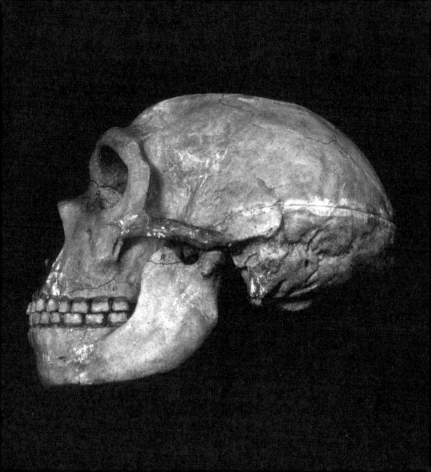

Ice ages

The Pleistocene era (beginning 2.58 million years ago) saw several phases in which Earth's mean temperature dropped and the polar icecaps expanded toward the tropics. These are clustered into four broad ice ages—periods with cool temperatures and a significant continental ice sheet (at times, up to one-third of Earth's land surface was covered), separated by interglacial periods of 10–15 millennia.

Nomadic humans, with fire, weapons, and language, were able to hunt across the tundra and secure caves in which to shelter. Their prey needed larger areas to forage, causing humanity to spread widely in pursuit. Falling sea levels opened up land bridges across today's oceans—most significantly, the Americas were populated by humans spreading from Mongolia, while horses evolved in America but migrated east before becoming extinct in their native land. The last significant glaciation came to an end 10,000 years ago, although a climatic cooling of about 500 years from *c*. AD 1300 has been noted.

Oceania

The Pacific Islands were unsettled by any of the early hominid species, but with assistance from ice-age land bridges, modern humans settled the Philippines, Australasia, and elsewhere by no later than 40,000 years ago (long after the earliest known boats). Eastern Polynesia may have been settled by South American sailors following the Humboldt Current. Sophisticated agriculture developed to supplement fishing.

The thousands of islands and huge ocean gulfs between them meant that settlement was uneven; some—such as Hawaii and Easter Island—remained unsettled until well into the first millennium AD. Isolation helped create significant linguistic diversity; there are not only hundreds of different languages, but several different language families (in civilizations without writing, oral histories were greatly developed). Philologists can chart the linguistic changes, dating the settlement of each island and tracking the rise and fall of loose-knit empires, with religiously potent chieftains and various class systems.

A plaster cast of an Arawi Maori shows detailed tribal tattoos—New Zealand was one of the last parts of Oceania to be settled by humans, about 800 years ago.

Neolithic expansion

At the end of the last ice age, humanity entered a period of increasing technological sophistication. For reasons that are still disputed, many of the large mammals hunted by humans became extinct, driving the development of new food sources: breadmaking considerably predates this period, but people in Mesopotamia now began cultivating wild cereal and legumes. Dogs had been domesticated over thousands of years; nomadic shepherding became possible through domestication of goats, sheep, horses, camels and, above all, cows.

By 5000 BC, livestock herding was sufficiently established to allow a widespread abandonment of hunter-gathering in favor of settled lifestyles. Pottery was increasingly useful, and permanent buildings, constructed from mudbrick, appeared. These technologies spread out of the Middle East through the Old World (the Americas developed agriculture independently, with only the llama available for domestication). With the arrival of bronze, stone was used less for tools and more for buildings.

Bronze and iron

The earliest manufactured alloy, bronze is made with copper and tin ores (and thus required trade with remote ore-producing regions). Gold and copper had previously been smelted, largely for decorative purposes, but bronze tools and weapons outlasted and outperformed stone. From c.3500 BC, their use spread from Mesopotamia, with different cultures amending recipes and techniques. The later discovery of similar techniques in the Americas seems unrelated.

Tools and swords that outlasted their owners made inheritance and theft possible, and as cities developed, so did professional armies. Fields could be ploughed and harrowed, and older clay and wax technologies were put to use in metal casting. Early experiments with iron ore produced a brittle, corroding metal, but around 610 BC, climate changes triggered mass migrations that made local iron ore mining in Europe easier than importing tin. Elsewhere, notably in Japan and southern Africa, bronze and iron arrived more or less simultaneously.

Mesopotamia

The Tigris and Euphrates rivers rise in the Taurus and Zagros mountains (modern-day Turkey and Iraq's Mosul region), flowing southeast to meet near Basra. The area between their near-parallel stretches was reliably fertile amid the surrounding desert, and gives rise to the Greek name "Mesopotamia." 10,000-year-old pottery from the region traces the southward movement of settled farms as the climate altered. The Neolithic discovery of mutant grasses with distended seeds that were easier to separate from their plants soon led to deliberate cultivation. Emmer wheat, rye, barley, and flax were selectively bred (though whether farmers realized this is debatable) and planted in oxen-ploughed fields. The advent of bronze made ploughing and harvesting less labor-intensive.

The need to predict and, to some extent, control water and crops tended toward priests, dynastic kings, and permanent farms specializing in single crops. Similar processes occurred in the Indus valley of India and the Yellow River in China (where the staple cereal was early rice). As rice reached Mesopotamia and India, while bronze reached China, it is tempting to assume some exchanges took place, but the pattern of development may be coincidence. Mesoamerica followed a similar pattern, also apparently independently. Townships became more durable and fortified: Susa, in Iran, and Ur, near the confluence of the rivers, were cities by *c.*4400 BC. Their bounty had to be recorded and protected, requiring both clerks and armies.

The earliest tallies were recorded as impressions in soft clay, from which the earliest known alphabets and arithmetic developed around 3100 BC—written "bustrophedon" alternated left-to-right and right-to-left, as a plough does in a field. Pictographic notes, running top-to-bottom, predate these. The written form of the Sumerian language, transcribed as if spoken, begins *c.*2600 BC; edicts and chronicles are accompanied by myths such as the Epic of Gilgamesh. The script takes decades to learn, suggesting that it was limited to a specialized cadre (including women, to begin with). Many other specialisms, notably architecture, carving, brewing, and metallurgy, can also be identified. One tantalizing detail: a female tavern-keeper, Kug-Bau, is listed as king of Sumer after 2500 BC, and later identified with various mother-goddesses.

Babylon

Despite its lack of native stone or wood, Mesopotamia gave rise to significant empires from populous cities such as Babylon, Ur, Jericho, Samara, and later Nineveh. Many of these empires are recalled as tyrannical (though of course records such as the Bible are history written by the vanquished).

Founded by Sumu-abum in 1894 BC, Babylon rose to imperial status under Hammurabi (1792–1750 BC). Many features of later cities developed here: written law, schools, taxes, stores, and traffic: wheels, originally used for pottery, were now so common on carts that roads were purpose-built. The Babylonian number system, based on divisions of 60, is still at the heart of our systems of geometry and timekeeping. Babylon ruled Mesopotamia for over a century, and later (after conquest by the Hittites, and Assyrian rule) was resurgent under Nebuchadnezzar II (634–562 BC), when it attacked Egypt and sacked Jerusalem, Tyre, and Nineveh. The reconstructed city and Hanging Gardens persisted for centuries.

Unified Egypt

Once agriculture arrived from Mesopotamia, Egyptian civilization evolved rapidly. It centered around the predictable regular flooding of the Nile River, which provided both irrigation and fertile silt. The Pharoah, treated as a living god, was supposed to ensure both sunrise and river tides through various rites, recorded in hieroglyphic ("priest-script") texts. Two major kingdoms developed: Lower Egypt around the Nile Delta, and Upper Egypt, bordering Sudan. Traditionally, the two were unified by the Pharaoh Menes around 3000 BC. Menes founded Egypt's First Dynasty (of 31 in total). Shortly thereafter, a new capital, Memphis, was built. Dynasties came and went frequently, with major regional conflicts and civil wars defining the Old, Middle, and New Kingdom periods.

The first step pyramid, built by the brilliant architect Imhotep about 2630 BC, was a natural progression of the mastaba tombs—Khufu's Great Pyramid, built a thousand years later, is the sole survivor of Herodotus's Seven Wonders of the World.

Judaism

Biblical accounts and archaeological findings are almost in accord: there were once two neighboring kingdoms, Judah in the south and Israel to the north, sharing the same monotheistic religion. Whether, as the Bible claims, Judah fell because of tolerance of other gods is unknown: current thinking is that it was a vassal state of Assyria. Therefore Babylon's king Nebuchadnezzar obliterated Judah's capital, Jerusalem (and its temple), around 600 BC, with a portion of its inhabitants taken into captivity. This exile inspired the formalization of the *Tanakh*, Jewish scriptures: much had already been written, but the canon was set at this period and shows signs of Babylonian cultural dominance.

Much of the population, however, had been left in Israel, causing conflict when Persian conqueror Cyrus the Great took Babylon and permitted the exiles to return to the Levant and rebuild their temple. Thereafter, Israel and Yehud (former Judah) would become increasingly self-reliant, gaining

independence again in the second century BC under
the Maccabees (the Selucid empire, who had succeeded the
Babylonians, were weakening). After the famous general
Pompey invaded in 63 BC, the area became Roman.

Following a great Jewish revolt, the second temple was
destroyed in the Roman sack of Jerusalem in AD 70, but Jewish
resistance to the Roman empire continued sporadically until
136 BC, when the Bar Koziba revolt against the violently anti-
Semitic Emperor Hadrian led to the dissolution of Israel and
the Diaspora (pan-European migration of Jews). Others had
moved eastward in Roman times, becoming useful contacts
for the Abbasid caliphate and Convivencia-era Spain, and
later Venice and the Ottoman empire. Talmudic commentary
and rabbinical lore would become vital mainstays of a faith
without a homeland. Christianity, meanwhile, was regarded as
an offshoot of Judaism until Constantine convened the Council
of Nicaea in AD 325. As Europe adopted this faith, migrant Jews
became convenient all-purpose hate-figures; the Black Death
was blamed on them and Tsarist pogroms forced many from
east Europe and Russia to America and east London in the
late 19th century. This trend, culminating in the Holocaust, led
to the creation of the modern state of Israel in 1948.

Minoan Crete

The largest Grecian island was home to the first significant Aegean civilization—the Bronze Age Minoan culture (approximately 27th –15th centuries BC). Like the Phoenicians, with whom they traded, they were skilled seafarers trading with Egypt and the Eastern Mediterranean; they had a written script known as Linear A, which is still untranslated today (Linear B seems to have been the first form of Greek). Many towns and palaces were built, the most famous of which, Knossos, inspired Greek myths of the labyrinth thanks to its sheer size, complexity, and religious rites involving bulls.

Minoan culture declined for a number of reasons—earthquakes affected the island more than once, and a natural disaster in the 15th century BC, possibly the eruption of the nearby Thera volcano, had a major impact. The cultural nexus now shifted toward the developing Mycenaean civilization of mainland Greece, but the tale of rapid destruction of a sophisticated civilization is sometimes credited with inspiring Plato's Atlantis.

Phoenicians

A group of Mediterranean seafaring city-states flourishing from c.1500 to 539 BC, the Phoenicians established many colonies, including Marseilles, Carthage, and Cadiz, but their power base was the Levant—roughly the modern-day Syrian and Lebanese coasts. Lacking natural resources aside from wood, they became superb sailors, shipwrights, and traders, gaining a reputation as successful if amoral merchants. Their Mediterranean "footprint" connected land routes from further afield, allowing silver, silk, ivory, murex shells, tin, glass, and ceramics to be ferried in their swift ships. They are generally credited with inventing the alphabet—rudimentary priestly systems existed for perhaps a millennium before the Phoenicians transcribed their Canaanite language c.1000 BC, but the phonetic nature of their version made it easy to transcribe new words, and trade allowed it to spread rapidly. Persia's Cyrus the Great conquered Phoenicia in 539 BC and Alexander the Great invaded in the fourth century BC (settling Sidon and Byblos peacefully, but massacring Tyre).

Akhenaten

Pharoah Amenhotep IV succeeded his father after a long and prosperous reign in 1353 BC. However, in the third year of his rule over Egypt, he renamed himself Akhenaten and decreed that all the anthropomorphic gods were subordinate to the disk of the Sun, Aten. Moreover, although the Pharoah was a living god, henceforth the entire royal family including his wive Nefertiti and children were to be deified. To facilitate this religious shift he established a new capital, Armarna, removing all nonAten iconography and commissioning curiously androgynous yet intimate depictions of the royal family.

Following a sudden death in 1340 BC, Akhenaten was erased from history until Armarna was rediscovered in 1714. His reign is followed by a four-year blank, during which Nefertiti may have ruled alone, before their frail son Tutankhamun, became the pawn of priests seeing a return to the old traditions. The few tantalizing fragments of his life that survive make Akhenaten a receptacle for diverse contemporary interpretations.

A highly stylized portrait of Akhenaten and his family.

Mesoamerican civilizations

Mesoamerica is the general term for an area comprising Mexico and Central America, and the civilizations found there. The Olmec (c.1200– 400 BC), developed many practices that came to characterize the region, including extensive trade networks, the calendar, handball games, stepped pyramids, and written glyphs (maize agriculture was already millennia old). They were followed by the city-states of the Mayans, who developed a numerical system, a full written language, and complex religion. This culture in turn began a gradual decline from the ninth century, when many of the southern cities were abandoned (perhaps due to a prolonged drought).

The northern Maya continued to flourish, while the Aztec empire (with a different language group and bloodier religious rites) sprang up in central Mexico around the 13th century. The Conquistadors would bring all this to a halt—the more diffuse Mayan culture survived Spanish incursion better than the Aztecs, and millions still speak Mayan languages today.

Assyria

This small Mesopotamian empire, bordering Babylon and the Hittite empire, went from consolidation to expansion under Tilgath-Pileser I (1174–1096 BC), then slumped. Assurnasipal II (883–859 BC) restored it, establishing Nineveh as the capital, while Salmaneser III (858–824 BC) expanded into Judah where he fought King Ahab. Tilgath-Pileser III (744–727 BC) captured Damascus and Gaza, reaching a compromise with Babylon.

The Assyrians pioneered displacement of conquered peoples: Sargon II, a general who rose to power rather than inheriting kingship, conquered Judah, parts of Egypt, and even Babylon, taking captives and tribute. Succession restored, Esarhaddon (680–669 BC) fought in Anatolia and resumed the Egyptian campaign. But after the capture of Thebes overextended the empire, his successor Assurbanipal faced internal strife and a rebellious Babylon. After Nebuchadnezzar II of Babylon married a Mede princess, the anti-Assyrian alliance captured Nineveh and ended the empire.

Iron

Remains of smithies and iron artefacts dating back to around 1700 BC have been found in India, Mesopotamia and Botswana, but these used pure iron from meteorites—refining of hematite began around 1300 BC. Purification of this iron ore was a laborious process and produced inferior metal; bronze was less brittle than early iron. However, the improved bloomery process needed less skill and resembled breadmaking or pottery; processing the resulting "pig-iron" into a durable metal entailed intensive hammering and forging. Oxidation had to be avoided, so the most popular technique used an enclosed clay kiln with charcoal to soak up impurities and oxygen. Reworked "wrought iron" was more ductile than cast iron.

Once these techniques were understood, iron could be made anywhere there was ore, mud, and wood, leather for a bellows and strong men with time on their hands (mythology and history show that the village smith was often a lame former soldier). Widespread ores made it more easily available than bronze.

Casting of molten iron in sand allowed for mass production of arrowheads and nails: such military iron was instrumental in the empire-building of Assyria, the Satavahana in central India and, later, the Han in China. Iron appears to have come late to China, around the start of the Warring States Era, but developed into sophisticated steel processing in the prosperous Wu state; its magnetic properties were observed there c. AD 100 and, eight centuries later, exploited with spoon-like compasses that always pointed north. Other countries, including Spain and Sri Lanka, created small quantities of steel by intensely reworking small amounts of iron—enough for Toledo daggers or Samurai swords, but not girders. Precise control of carbon impurities was the key ingredient, allowing for much stronger alloys.

The mass production of steel from hitherto unusable ore changed the world, enabling the age of steam, large-scale factory-based production, the superior ploughs that drove the Agrarian Revolution, and even the exploration of space. Steel allowed the construction of skyscrapers, sterilizable surgical instruments, cables, and precision components. High-performance engines became possible, as did everything from high-quality flatware to refrigeration.

Roman Republic

The foundation of Rome is traditionally dated to 753 BC—in myth, it is attributed to the twins Romulus and Remus, and it is fairly certain that a monarchy did indeed begin around this date. At the time, Etruscan culture flourished in northern Italy —the new kingdom remained relatively minor until 509 BC, when the tyrant Tarquin was overthrown (legendarily due to his rape of Lucrece) and the Republic was founded under two consuls.

The famous Senate was not especially democratic, but began a tradition of nonmonarchical rule that, combined with the precedent of the Greeks, would have a great influence on the Enlightenment. Rome became a great military power, with a standing army of legionaries—the attempt of one Greek general to attack Italy gave the world the "Pyrrhic victory," while Rome's greatest rival, Carthage, was soundly defeated in the Punic Wars. By the time of Julius Caesar, the Republic had control of the Mediterranean Sea, ruled territories from Iberia to Macedon, and had taken North Africa.

Now in ruins, the Forum was the heart of public life in the Roman Republic.

Buddhism

Gautama Siddhartha, (*c.*563–483 BC) was an Indian noble who, tradition records, became a monk after his first observance of others suffering. Whereas Hinduism holds that reincarnation is determined by actions in each life (*karma*), Gautama, the "Buddha" (enlightened one), advocated using a human life to break free of this eternal cycle and achieve *nirvana* (oblivion). Thereafter, he traveled widely, guiding others onto his "Eightfold Path." Other Buddhas have followed, as well as bodhisattvas, individuals who forestall their personal *nirvana* in order to guide others.

Buddhism spread slowly through Asia: its essentially flexible structure meant that it was compatible with many other faiths (including Hinduism, although Buddhism fell from favor in its homeland following the Safavid conquests). China in particular adopted it, incorporating practices from Lao Tzu and other Taoist sages to produce Zen Buddhism. Today, it has millions of practitioners around the world.

Thermopylae

Persian king Darius's attempt to subjugate Greece ended in Athenian victory at Marathon in 490 BC. Ten years later his son Xerxes I prepared a huge army (Greek historian Herodotus says several million; in reality, at least 100,000).

Some 7,000 volunteers, including the fabled 300 Spartans led by Leonidas (opposite), were sent to the narrow Thermopylae pass, the route from northern to southern Greece, correctly anticipating Xerxes' tactics. The phalanxes held and inflicted severe casualties on the Persians (including Xerxes' elite "Immortals" and two of his brothers) with minimal losses until the third day, when they were betrayed and outflanked. Xerxes was uncharacteristically merciless to the survivors. Reports of the Spartans' valor inspired the Greek resistance. The Persians took most of Greece before the Battle of Salamis (a naval conflict largely lost by Xerxes' poor tactics). A united Greece prevailed—yet a generation later, Sparta would enlist Persian help in the Peloponnesian Wars against Athens.

Warring States Era

Following China's "Spring and Autumn" period of city-states in conflict, a phase of larger states vying for power resulted in a unified China. By 475 BC, there were six large states surrounding five smaller, better-resourced ones. The last to emerge, Qin, began on the southwestern extreme, but by 220 BC these "barbarians" were, briefly, overall rulers.

During this period Sun Tsu wrote *The Art of War*; chariots were supplanted by cavalry, and iron swords and arrows. In 453 BC, Han, Zhao, and Wei states conquered the Zhi dynasty in the Battle of Jinyang, splitting the super-state of Jin into three. A century later, Wei princeling Shan Yan became prime minister of Qin and revolutionized it with draconian laws and Legalism, a rigidity fused with Confucian philosophy. His ferociously trained army proved to be his nemesis, but from 269-230 BC, Qin built up forces and supply chains that ultimately allowed Shi Huang, the first emperor, to control the whole of China. Following his death in 210 BC, the Han rapidly wrested control.

Lao Tzu

The influential work known as the *Tao Te Ching (or Dao De Jing)* is one of many religious, philosophical, and cultural developments of the sixth century BC (Buddhism, Confucianism, Zoroastrianism, and the Ramayana date from this period). It may be the work of one man or an entire tradition, but it is usually attributed to Lao Tzu (Lao Tse or Laozi: "Old Master").

Taoism interprets the universe in cyclic processes rather than eternal states, and seeks to disregard apparent distinctions; polarities (male/female, hard/soft, light/dark, Yin/Yang) are tendencies, not absolutes. To become closer to the *Tao* (way, flow) is to *be* something rather than *do* it. After Buddhism arrived in China following the collapse of the Han dynasty (c. AD 220), a Taoist-inflected Buddhism, Zen, developed. Taoism also concerns the flow of essential energy, *chi*, and underlies practices including acupuncture, Feng-Shui, and Tai-Chi: misinterpretation of the latter regimen caused Westerners to identify a 19th-century revolt as the "Boxer Rebellion."

Plato and Aristotle

Two great Athenian pilosophers developed radically differing approaches: much later European thought is a debate between these two poles. Plato (c.424–347 BC) wrote many dialogues—fictional conversations, generally with his mentor Socrates, in which leading questions guide the hapless pupil (himself) to infer truths from his own logical deduction—the Socratic method. His most famous work, *The Republic*, mused on the nature of an ideal state. He founded the Academy, which trained thinkers until the Roman conquest of Athens. On Plato's death, Aristotle (384–322 BC) left the Academy and abandoned its main teaching (that the material world was an approximation of transcendent truth) in favor of close examination of nature. He wrote extensively, tutored Alexander the Great and developed Plato's ideas of deduction into formal logic. This led him to posit identifiable, systematic patterns of a natural order: science. Much of his work is lost, but medieval theologians would accept his preserved ideas unquestioningly, while failing to uphold his respect for rational inquiry.

Plato (left) and
Aristotle, depicted
in Raphael's fresco
The School of Athens.

Confucianism and the bureaucratic state

Kong Fuzi ("Master Kong," anglicized to "Confucius") lived in the Lu kingdom (modern Shandong) 551–479 BC. Whereas Buddhism sees this world as a distraction from truth and Lao Tzu sought to connect conduct in this life with the cosmic, Confucianism sees meritorious conduct and social harmony as quasi-spiritual observances and ends in themselves. Kong Fuzi grew up amid social upheaval and rather than rely on divine protection, believed that mutual aid was the will of heaven; this led him to emphasize the family unit. In his peripatetic teaching and arguments for respect and close observation, he was analogous to Aristotle and, like him, advocated a methodology at odds with the dogmatism of later followers. In the Han era, his *Analects* were used to prevent social mobility and operate a scholastic system that took decades to train an official. A vast empire put all its effort into homeostasis, with more clerks than soldiers: some have argued that Mao could not have established control so rapidly had China not spent two millennia governed on these lines.

至聖孔子

名丘字仲尼山東
兗州府曲阜縣人

Alexander the Great

Son of the ambitious King Philip II of Macedon, Alexander (356–323 BC) was hugely influenced by his tutor Aristotle. On accession to the throne in 336, he set about spreading Hellenistic thinking and influence through invasion; he reached as far afield as India, and after conquering the ancient kingdom of Egypt he founded the new city of Alexandria as the focus of his empire. He set the template for charismatic conquerors, fostering legends and an iconography later invoked by everyone from Lord Byron and Napoleon to John F. Kennedy. Greek became the universal language of learning, even well into Roman times. The story about his weeping because he had conquered everything already is misleading—near the end of his life, he was planning to invade the Arabian desert.

After his death (possibly poisoning, but very likely illness), his empire quickly broke apart. Yet the smaller successor states would prove more stable—the Ptolemies in Egypt would persist until Julius Caesar, the Selucids in the Middle East even longer.

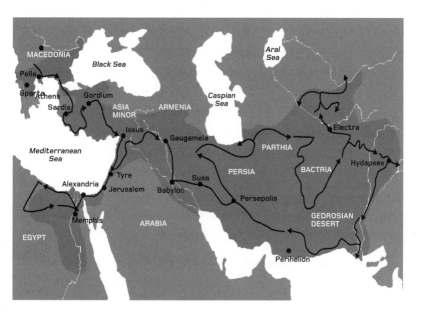

This map shows Alexander's campaigns from 336–323 BC, with darker areas outlining the extent of his empire.

Ashoka

Chandragupta Maurya unified most of India by expansion of the Nanda empire that Alexander's men had refused to invade. Maurya's son expanded further, and *his* son Ashoka (*c*. 304–232 BC) ruled an empire that stretched across the subcontinent from Persia to Bengal. The major exception was the democratic Kalinga state, which Ashoka went onto conquer in a war so bloody that he repented and became a Buddhist. Hinduism was then the main religion, while Buddhism was relatively young: Ashoka's conversion was as significant as Emperor Constantine's later endorsement of Christianity.

Ashoka became a much-beloved ruler, ordering the cessation of sacrifices (he stipulated that cows be protected), tree-planting, and erection of stone markers with dictates for his subjects that have been a boon to later archaeologists. However, the empire barely outlived him, and India was not reunified until the time of the Mughals, though the fourth to sixth century AD Gupta empire came close.

Ashoka erected pillars such as this one across his kingdom, commemorating locations in the life of the Buddha and his own royal visits.

Carthage and the Punic Wars

The Roman Republic's greatest rival in its initial struggle for power was Carthage, a wealthy port in present-day Libya. As the only two powers strong enough to control the Mediterranean, they fought to determine who would do so. *Cartaga Delenda Est*—"Carthage must be destroyed"—was the most potent rallying cry of any Roman city and the rivalry passed into myth with the story of Dido and Aeneas.

Carthage had the stronger navy, but Rome stole their designs; in land engagements, Rome generally proved victorious. The Punic Wars lasted more than a century (264–146 BC, with interruptions). During the second war, Carthaginian general Hannibal Barca led a force equipped with war-elephants from his family's base in southern Spain to northern Italy across the Alps: he stayed in Italy for 15 years, capturing various cities, but never managed to sack Rome. The third war was a mere siege, ending with total Roman dominance and Carthage's destruction (the strategically useful port was rebuilt later).

Celts

The Celts were a European tribal culture, bound together not by politics but language and tradition, whose heyday was during the last millennium BC. Polytheistic and warfaring, they seem to have emerged in central Europe, and at their fullest expansion reached into France, Spain, and eventually Britain (Stonehenge was built 2,000 or more years before Celtic druids; Roman historians got this and much else wrong.)

The Roman empire's expansion assimilated many (the Gauls fought by Julius Caesar were Celtic, and readily took to Roman culture—Caesar recorded the story about them wearing blue woad into battle). Expansion by Germanic tribes further diminished their lands, so that by the downfall of the Roman empire, the Celts remained only in Brittany (northwest France) and the British Isles. Nevertheless, this cultural legacy would greatly shape resistance to the Norman invaders of 1066 and beyond—Wales, Ireland, Cornwall, and Scotland all preserve Celtic identity, if not genes.

Great Wall of China

For millennia various walls had been built across northern China to protect fertile croplands from nomadic tribes and symbolically demark the boundaries of civilization. The first emperor, Shi Huang, ordered they be combined into a greater whole after the Warring States Era, and General Meng Tian duly began construction of the Yellow River defenses in 215 BC.

Originally built from packed earth, in the 14th century the Ming dynasty rebuilt sections with brick or stone—thousands of miles, at least one story high (the Ming, who supplanted the Mongol Yuan dynasty founded by Kublai Khan, had good reason to fear invasion). The Wall's significance as a border line persisted into the 20th century. The Japanese invasion of Manchuria in 1931 continued for two years until successfully breaching the defenses at the Wall, but stopped there. General Chiang Kai-shek signed the Tanggu Truce calling for a demilitarized zone around the wall, and Japan kept control of Manchuria through the second Sino-Japanese War.

Julius Caesar

A brilliant military strategist and statesman (100–44 BC), Gaius Julius Caesar's first brush with politics came when his uncle lost a civil war to Sulla, Rome's first dictator since the Punic Wars. Caesar fled Rome, joined the army and, after Sulla's death, returned to be elected tribune. His political career flourished and in 59 BC he became a consul in the First Triumvirate—a power-sharing arrangement with bitter rivals Pompey and Crassus. He swiftly conquered Gaul and became its governor (mounting an expedition to Britain in 55 BC), before returning to Rome with his army (crossing into Italy at the Rubicon River). Crassus had already been defeated in Parthia, but Pompey fled to Alexandria, prompting the Fall of Egypt.

Caesar became dictator, soon voted into office for life. His enemies, alarmed at his growing power, assassinated him at the Senate on the Ides of March, but the resulting civil war, ironically, led to his heir Octavius becoming emperor, and the name "Caesar" denoting the imperial title for many centuries.

The Fall of Egypt

Amid the breakup of the Macedonian empire, Alexander the Great's general Ptolemy established a new dynasty in Egypt, with Alexandria as its capital. Despite bitter conflict with the Selucids (Persian Macedonians), internal harmony prevailed—the Ptolemies encouraged native culture, and the Rosetta Stone was carved in honor of Ptolemy V's coronation. The Roman Republic had always been tempted by this rich land, and after Pompey's conflict with Julius Caesar went awry, he sought asylum in Egypt. Here, Cleopatra VII was locked in civil war with her brother Ptolemy XIII, who assassinated Pompey to win Caesar's favor; Caesar pondered conquest, before supporting Cleopatra (they became lovers). Cleopatra also charmed Roman general Mark Antony, who came to Egypt after Caesar's death, maintaining Egyptian independence until Caesar's heir Augustus (né Octavius) arrived with his fleet. Egypt's forces were destroyed in the Battle of Actium (31 BC), and Antony and Cleopatra committed suicide. Egypt became a prosperous province with Alexandria as a seat of learning.

The *Pax Romana*

Soon after the Fall of Egypt, Julius Caesar's heir Octavius was declared Emperor Augustus, transforming the Roman Republic into an empire. For the first two centuries of the modern era, Rome enjoyed an unprecedented period of peace and consolidation. Eventually reaching from Britain to Judea, the empire depended on slaves, but was multicultural, succeeding in large part because it encouraged assimilation of newly subjugated states: a citizen of Rome was a citizen, regardless of origin or posting. The state religion was flexible enough to accommodate almost any faith (barring the monotheistic Jews and early Christians). The Sassanian empire to the east was its only substantial rival, and despite conflicts, they maintained trading relations. Germanic tribes began pushing at the frontier (the river Rhine) in the third century, but Rome was still dominant when Emperor Diocletian divided the empire in 293; Constantine would temporarily reverse this, but the western half ultimately fell to Alaric and Attila the Hun. Byzantium endured until the Fall of Constantinople.

Aksumite empire

Ethiopia was a rich land, with fertile soil and a position on the Red Sea ideal for traders. The early D'mt kingdom gave way to smaller states after about AD 500, but an empire based in Axum, northern Ethiopia, later reunited the region, developing sophisticated trade and ruling an area that at times included Yemen, parts of Egypt, and Djibouti. Between AD 100 and 500 it was a significant power, a conduit for minerals, ivory, and spices.

Axum's commercial use of Greek and Semitic languages and minted coins led some scholars to assume that Axum was an outpost of another power, but its written archives and architecture, including distinctive towering stelae, counter such allegations (though legends connect it to the Ark of the Covenant and the Queen of Sheba). From 300, the power base moved south to the confluence of the Nile. King Ezana made Coptic Christianity the state religion after 330, and stories of an unknown Christian state later encouraged European explorers. Early Muslim refugees, however, found shelter here.

Constantine

Born in AD 272, Constantine rose from humble origins to become one of the last rulers of the unified Roman empire. His influential mother, Helena, was reputedly a concubine, though little is known about her except that she made the first Christian pilgrimage. The empire was already splitting into East and West as he rose to power, and his decision to base imperial operations in Byzantium (renamed Constantinople) enabled a form of Roman rule to continue until the city's Fall in 1453. He was a strong general, reversing Germanic incursions on Roman territory, but died in 337, before taking on the Sassanians.

Constantine attributed his abrupt success to Christianity, made it the *de facto* state religion and ordered various church councils. The creed developed at the Council of Nicaea remains the definitive explication of Christian belief (see the Schism). The Arian heresy, with its contentious doubts about the Trinity, was officially repudiated there, but various Germanic tribes, including the Visigoths, adopted Arianism anyway.

Sassanian empire

Following their defeat by Alexander the Great, the Persians regrouped under the aegis of the Parthians and opposed the Romans and Arabs for four centuries. A new dynasty, founded by Ardashir I, ruled and extended the empire—at its peak, it incorporated Afghanistan, Alexandria, Cappadocia, and Albania. The Sassanid purlieu included the Indian Ocean and the Silk Road and formed a mirror of Rome—indeed, in AD 253 an abortive counterstrike after Sassanian forces took Antioch saw the capture of Emperor Valerian, who died in captivity.

As the center of Roman power moved east to Byzantium, the empires were defined by mutual antagonism. Nevertheless, as Shungnu (Hun) nomads purged from China surged west, Rome and Persepolis reached a pact in 387. However, fresh assaults by Emperor Heraclius in the seventh century depleted the Sassanian forces and exchequer. He engineered internal power struggles, aided by a plague that killed the Shah and half the population, permitting the Muslim Arab conquest of 636.

The remains of the mud-brick fort of Narin Qal'eh at Meybod in modern Iran are dated to the Sassanian era.

Abyssinian empire

The Aksumite empire had expanded into Arabia, but with the advent of Islam it declined after the sixth century. Poor harvests, an overextended army, and the Sassanid conquests in Egypt weakened the state, and by the tenth century it was back to almost its original boundaries. The Aksumite kings were overthrown by Queen Gudit. The Zagwe dynasty came to power in the north, establishing Abyssinia and ruling until 1270, when the Solomonic dynasty took control, trying not always successfully to unite the various kingdoms (some now Islamic).

Portuguese explorers arrived in 1490, and missionaries followed. In 1529, the Ottomans invaded to support local Muslims, but with Portuguese help, the Solomonic cause succeeded at the 1543 Battle of Wayna Daga. The country fell into civil war in 1769 and was only reunited in 1855 by Emperor Tewodros II. He and his successors stabilized and modernized the region, allowing it to resist Italian colonization. The Solomonic dynasty only ended with the 1974 communist overthrow of Emperor Haile Selassie.

Rumors of the Abyssinian Empire reaching Europe inspired medieval belief in the mythical Christian kingdom of Prester John, as depicted on this Renaissance map.

Alaric

In AD 408 the Visigoths, one of many Germanic tribes that had been harassing the Roman Empire, penetrated to its original heart. By this time, Rome was no longer the official capital—Emperor Diocletian had moved it when he split the empire into West and East. Visigoth leader Alaric I had formerly cooperated with the Romans, even serving as a Roman soldier. He laid siege to Rome in AD 408, extracted a heavy toll for leaving, then returned and finished the job in 410. Little wreckage occurred, but the city was stripped of valuables and all barbarian slaves were freed. Alaric died of illness that same year.

One side effect of the defense of Italy was the withdrawal of frontier troops, which meant abandoning the Rhine and other outlying territories. The empire's decline was a slow process that finally ended in the Fall of Constantinople. Yet the sack of Rome by Goths, Vandals, and others precipitated the collapse of Western Europe and land-grabs by Attila the Hun, Genghis Khan, Saxons, Vikings, Franks, Normans, and the Umayyad caliphs.

Shinto

Unlike China, Japan only gained writing relatively recently. The first records date to the fourth or fifth century AD, and earlier historical information is limited. Japan was unified in the fourth century, under an imperial dynasty (traditionally dated to the sixth century BC, but probably founded around this time). A series of military leaders—shoguns—were in control by the 12th century AD, and soon after, the country fell into feudal conflict.

Japan's native belief system, Shinto, revolves around spirits, rituals to please them and shrines in their honor. Despite attempts to make it a state religion, it is as much a series of cultural practices as a faith, and historically has flourished harmoniously alongside other religions (especially Buddhism). Two foundational works, the eighth-century *Kojiki* and *Nihon Shoki*, purport to explain the history of Japan up to the time of writing. They distil oral myth from much older traditions, starting with the creation myth and ending with the thoroughly historical Empress Jito.

Silk Road

India, China, and Europe were dimly aware of each other before Alexander's eastern ventures. Silk had reached Rome from the east, but its origins were unknown. The passage of goods accelerated with the end of the Warring States Era as the Han, desperate for good horses, exchanged their most valuable assets with traders to the west of their borders. Individual expeditions would make parts of the journey, trading their wares with others who had traversed a different section; it was rare for individuals to make the complete transasiatic journey. Parties would band together for safety in caravans of horses, camels, or yaks, especially once the Huns began raiding.

The term "Silk Road" is a 19th-century misnomer; there were in fact many origins and destinations, three land routes and several sea routes. Some caravans took the southern routes, to or from Mesopotamia via the Karakorum mountains and the Hindu Kush; some went north around the desolate Taklamakan Desert and Afghanistan. Others traversed the Ganges Delta to reach what is now Bangladesh, then turned north. Sailors from Sri Lanka traded with the Aksumite empire, who took goods north. Constantinople was a significant focus, but the Abbasid caliphate sought to dominate the western margin of the route as the Tang dynasty grew in confidence.

Spices were increasingly important to northern Europeans, both for status and as a means to make preserved meat palatable. Herbs were used for medicine; lapis lazuli for icons. Information flowed, techniques passed between continents: "Arabic" numbers and the compass spread from India, Islam went there via the Sassanid empire. Buddhism and some later Assyrian Christians reached China. The stories told by and to traders passed back to Europe without verification: tales of the Christian Emperor Prester John and Sir John Mandeville's preposterous stories were taken seriously for centuries; Marco Polo's accounts have lately been questioned, but provide a summary of what was known by Western travelers.

With the rise of the Ming dynasty, the Fall of Constantinople, and Europe's increasing skill at navigation, the importance of the Silk Road diminished after 1500, altering power balances in the area (notably the Safavid and Mughal empires).

St. Augustine

The Christian church developed from a small Jewish cult in the first century AD, to an empire-spanning religion by the fourth. Perhaps the most important theologian in the immediate wake of Constantine's decision to make Christianity the Roman state religion, was Augustine (354–430), whose doctrines would shape Christianity to the Reformation and beyond.

Born in Roman North Africa, Augustine's early life was given over to lurid hedonism until a spontaneous, passionate conversion, described in his autobiographical *Confessions*. He struggled with these impulses for the rest of his life, and as a result of his influence a misogynistic streak has forever colored Church doctrine on women. The doctrine of original sin (humans are born sinful, requiring baptism) was largely his formulation, and the biblical canon was decided under his aegis. His *City of God*, written after Alaric's sack of Rome, emphasized the afterlife over worldly concerns, and outlined the theory of "just war" (later used to justify the Crusades and much else).

Attila the Hun

Leader of an empire that rose and fell with his reign—his date of birth is uncertain, but he ruled between AD 434 and 453. The early history of the Huns is unclear; they may be the Xiongnu people purged from Mongolia by the Han Chinese. They enter written history as nomadic warfaring tribes in the 300s, with sophisticated mounted archery techniques. Their encroachment on Europe pushed the Germanic tribes in turn toward Roman territory. Both halves of the Roman empire found it useful to pay tribute and employ them as mercenaries.

Attila had greater ambitions—with his brother Bleda he invaded the Byzantine empire, forcing the emperor to sign a humiliating peace agreement and agree to increase tribute payments. Repeating the process, Attila nearly took Constantinople, but after Bleda's death in 445, he turned to the Western empire, reaching Orléans and Milan. The emperor sent Pope Leo I to lead negotiations, which succeeded (unlike those with Alaric's Visigoths). Attila died before he could mount another attempt.

Islam

Muhammad (c.570–632) was a caravan trader who became the prophet of Islam—a monotheistic religion rooted in Judaeo-Christian tradition—and a successful war leader. By the time of his death, Arabia (including the holy cities of Mecca and Medina) was united under the new faith, but factionalism now led to civil wars. The Shi'a believed in divine inspiration of Muhammad's family, supporting his son-in-law Ali (credited with inspiring the mystical tradition of Sufism), and later his grandson Hussain. The Sunni, meanwhile, believed that caliphs ("successors") should be communal leaders, exemplars of doctrinal knowledge and faith. When Hussain was decapitated in the 680 Battle of Karbala, attempting reconciliation with the Umayyad caliph, his martyrdom forever split the two parties. Internal conflict did not stop external conquest; by 730 the Umayyad caliphate reached from Iberia to India. Modern Iran is Shi'a, but as Persia it was a Sunni stronghold. The Mughals and Ottomans were Sunni. Wahhabi Sunni forces of the House of Saud suppressed popular Shi'ism in Arabia after 1744.

An Lushan Rebellion

A half-Sogdian foundling, An Lushan became a general and found favor from the Tang emperor, Xuanzong. However, during the power struggle surrounding Xuanzong's favorite concubine (Yang Guifei, subject of many romances) and her ambitious brother (or cousin), An Lushan opted to rebel, possibly for his own safety, proclaiming himself emperor of a Yen dynasty in AD 755. He captured the western city of Loyang before assaulting the vast capital of Chang'an. On the condition that he killed Guifei and her brother/cousin, Xuanzong was finally able to lead his own troops against the rebellion, bolstered by Turkish mercenaries.

An was killed by his son two years into the seven-year revolt, but the convulsions devastated China for generations. Millions died and many more fled south, making precise estimates of the death toll impossible: 36 million are unaccounted for±one-sixth of the global population at the time. In the aftermath, the formerly cosmopolitan Tang turned inward for centuries.

Abbasid caliphate

The Umayyad caliphate extended the power of Arabic Islam, but one family, descended from al-Abbas, gained support from the Umayyads' Shi'a and Persian rivals before attacking outright in AD 750. A major disagreement was the status of Arab Muslims relative to recent converts; the Abbasids were more tolerant. They established Baghdad as a new power base and Basra as a focus of learning. Persia's wealth and culture shifted the new regime toward the Sunni and incorporated Sassanian law. Significantly, the empire was based on Islamic rather than Arabic identity. Caliph Abu al-Abbas as-Saffah encroached on Uzbekistan, confronting China's Tang. There was also conflict with Constantinople (whose conquest, it was claimed, would confirm messianic prophesies).

The seeds of Abbasid downfall were sown in their reliance on Mamluks who increasingly took control, and in 1258, the Mongol siege of Baghdad ended with the trampling of the last Abbasid caliph to control an empire, though they ruled Cairo until 1517.

ABASSID CALIPHS

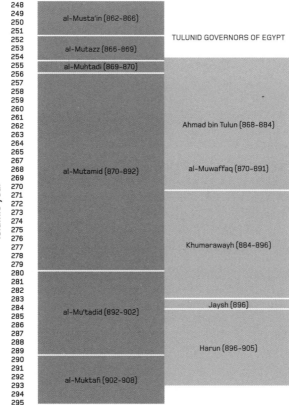

Islamic year

248–251 al-Musta'in (862–866)	
	TULUNID GOVERNORS OF EGYPT
252–254 al-Mutazz (866–869)	
255 al-Muhtadi (869–870)	
	Ahmad bin Tulun (868–884)
al-Mutamid (870–892)	al-Muwaffaq (870–891)
	Khumarawayh (884–896)
al-Mu'tadid (892–902)	Jaysh (896)
	Harun (896–905)
al-Muktafi (902–908)	

Native Americans

Indigenous North American cultures tended to be more tribal than the Mesoamerican or Inca cultures, with hundreds of different languages. The eastern Mississippians, known for their earthern mounds, were one dominant culture. Developing c. AD 700, they were characterized by theocratic chieftains and settled agriculture around rivers (corn from the south was a staple crop, along with beans and squashes). They congregated in the southeast and Midwest; Mesoamerican obsidian found in Wisconsin has proved trading links across the continent.

Drought and European settlement had deleterious effects; the indigenous cultures all suffered from the introduction of European diseases such as smallpox, as well as warfare with the new arrivals. The Great Plains tribes fought wars with the Conquistadors, but were energized by the introduction of the horse, which encouraged bison hunting over subsistence agriculture. Like the eastern farmers, they lost their lands to the growing United States.

Charlemagne

The Frankish tribes reclaimed many of Imperial Rome's former territories under Pepin the Short, who donated lands to the church in return for papal approval of his *de facto* kingship. Pepin's elder son, Charles (born *c*. AD 740), inherited half the kingdom in 768, and the remainder after his brother Carloman's abrupt death three years later. He expanded his dominance of Western Europe to include Bohemia, Saxony, northern Spain, and Lombardy. He consolidated a legal and commercial code, standardizing measures, but was mainly concerned with the promulgation of Catholicism.

In exchange, Pope Leo III crowned him Holy Roman Emperor over Christmas 800—the title conferred no new powers, but great prestige: even Constantinople now turned to Charles in resolving factional disputes and countering Haroun al-Rashid. He died in 814, buried in Aachen. Later rulers sought to emulate or link themselves with him, and it was Frederic Barbarossa who coined the name Charlemagne (Charles the Great).

Saxons

One of many itinerant Germanic tribes jockeying for status in the post-Roman power vacuum, the Saxons were based around where modern Denmark and Germany meet (not quite today's "Saxony"). As with the Vikings, they barely acknowledged distinctions between trade and pillage. When ranging south they encountered the Franks and were, eventually, converted and subsumed by Charlemagne in the late eighth century. Well before this, they installed themselves as rulers across much of Britain (legendarily, after being invited in as mercenaries).

Fewer moved west than has been thought, but as traders they had superior goods and a more useful language, and within a century they, the Angles and Jutes had influenced British natives enough to confuse future archeologists. Among the warlords, however, Anglo-Saxon blood and culture mingled with Celtic and Romano-British. Ultimately, these Saxons also converted to Christianity and, faced with Viking invaders, united under Alfred the Great of the kingdom of Wessex in the 880s.

Haroun al-Rashid

Even before becoming fifth Abbasid caliph in 786, Haroun "the Just" had learned to delegate: his Barmakid clients ran parts of his empire as franchises, increasing his wealth but diminishing direct control. Instead, Haroun advocated learning, culture, and contact with other empires, sending emissaries to Charlemagne and Tang China, establishing Baghdad as a metropolis, and founding the *Bayt al-Hikma* library. While many fables attach themselves to him, the gifts he sent Charlemagne were just as wonderful as claimed, and included a mechanical clock that was returned for resembling sorcery. From the Tang he took the secret of paper, making Persian culture more exportable and adding to his prestige. He also came the closest of any caliph to taking Constantinople.

On his death, his sons al-Amin and al-Ma'Mun split the empire and fought for overall control. This, and the system of regional governance, weakened the caliphate, making Haroun's reign a high-water mark. The *1001 Nights* has reinforced this impression.

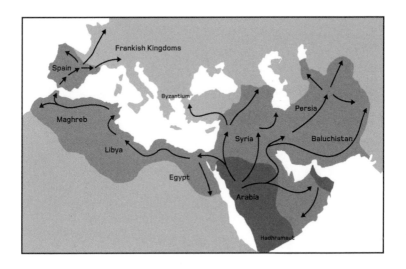

| | Islamic world by death of Muhammad, 632 | | Islamic world by c.750 | | Non-Islamic areas |

Vikings and Rus

Tribes from Denmark and Scandinavia took advantage of disarray among their rivals to sail into profitable lands in search of trade and plunder. Those who went west became known as "Vikings," while eastward parties moving down the Volga toward Constantinople were dubbed "Rus." Both names recall fine seamanship: their longboats were maneuverable and sometimes light enough to carry between rivers. The Rus traded slaves, silver, and glass for amber, fur, and wool, founded Kiev as a way station, and brought silk from Baghdad. The Vikings colonized Greenland, Iceland, and America, as well as raiding and settling Saxon England.

One posited reason for this expansionism is a fear that their way of life was jeopardized by the spread of Catholicism in Europe: the runic alphabet was deemed unholy, and conversion was part of Alfred the Great's campaign to oust Vikings from England. Raids became sporadic after AD 900, but they left behind words, tombs, and chess (though not horned helmets).

La Convivencia

The Umayyad Arabs led an initial Islamic surge of conquest that reached Iberia before Charles Martel (Charlemagne's grandfather) halted further expansion at the 732 Battle of Tours. Thus North African proselytes brought Arabic influence to Spain and Portugal, venturing as far as Marseilles and Pamplona. El Andaluz, as it became, was a refuge of the Umayyads from the Abbasid caliphate, but allowed Persian art and ideas, remnants of classical scholarship, and fresh learning from India and China to mix with Christian European culture. Whether its citizens coexisted so easily is debatable.

The cities of Toledo and Seville became powerhouses of ideas. Arabic wind power and plumbing, plus refined Greek research, allowed irrigation and architecture on vast scales; automata later became the stuff of fairy tales, and surgery was centuries ahead of Europe's. A drip-feed of Moorish learning caused a minor renaissance in 13th-century Europe, but after 1492, Jews and Moors were evicted by Ferdinand and Isabella.

Lindisfarne Gospels

The kingdoms that would form England became Christian in a piecemeal fashion. Northumbria, on the Scottish border, had many monasteries, and Lindisfarne, home of St. Cuthbert, was a site of pilgrimage and power. Mostly illiterate congregations were exposed to magnificent icons, one of which—a copy of the Gospels—survived Vikings, Normans, and the 1536 Reformation.

Probably inscribed by Bishop Eadfrith at the start of the eighth century, the illustrations and ornamentation reveal influence from Germanic, Greek Orthodox, Celtic, and Arabic sources, while inlaid lapis lazuli, indigo, and gold show trade links to the Himalayas and North Africa. Some pages include meticulous pointillist lead-work, reflecting the nature of such books as acts of devotion as much as objects to be read. When seen closeup the detail of the decoration is analogous to an Eastern mandala. Over two centuries later, Bishop Aldred added a glossary in the demotic text, making this the earliest known English-language translation of the Gospels.

incipit euangelii
genelogia mathei

LIB ER

GENERATI
ONISIHU
XPIFILIIDAUID
FILII ABRAHAM

Twelver Shi'ism

After Islam split into Sunni (the majority) and Shi'a, each developed internal sects. The most influential among the Shi'a were the Twelvers, who believe that Muhammad's family provided 12 great imams (holy leaders), exemplifying the faith. The 11th imam, Hasan ibn Ali, died c. AD 874, and according to Twelvers, his infant son Muhammad ibn Hasan was hidden by Allah from the Abbasid caliphate. Becoming incorporeal to influence the world as pure spirit, he will return at the end of the world as the Mahdi (redeemer). Sunni Muslims believe the Mahdi is yet to come—or never will.

Although not all Shi'a accept this, the sect has been powerful; Persia's Safavid dynasty adopted it, forming a historical legacy for the ayatollahs of modern Iran. Shi'a countries have more influential clergy than Sunni countries, with religious leaders acting as state leaders. Persian influence in India established Twelvers as an important minority there, despite Mughal opposition. A self-proclaimed Mahdi ruled Sudan from 1881–85.

Normans

A Viking war leader known as Rollo (c. AD 846–931) conquered portions of Frankish territory in northern France and, after negotiating terms with the Carolingian king, founded the semiautonomous Duchy of Normandy in 911. It quickly became one of the most powerful in the realm. The Normans retained their seafaring proclivities; one group conquered southern Italy, forming the Kingdom of Sicily, besieging

Constantinople, and vying for control of the Mediterranean. Holy Roman Emperor Henry VI married into the family, then absorbed it in 1194.

The Norman dukes also married into England's Saxon royalty, giving William the Bastard (c.1028–87) a hereditary claim to the throne. His army defeated the other claimant (and last Saxon king) Harold Godwinson in the 1066 Battle of Hastings, giving him the more famous appellation of "the Conqueror." Norman nobles became the English aristocracy, and English kings would retain their Norman holdings for centuries—their vivid memory would contribute to the Hundred Years' War.

Schism

Christianity had suffered internal conflict in its first thousand years—heresies such as Arianism (that Jesus had been created instead of existing eternally) led to grave disputes. Yet theoretically it had remained unified until 1054, the traditional date for the schism between the Roman Catholic and the Eastern Orthodox churches. The division of the Roman empire had led to a spilt in religious practices as well and theological agreement had failed in the ninth century. In 1053, the Patriarch of Constantinople (the Eastern capital),

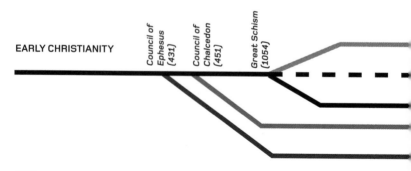

EARLY CHRISTIANITY

Council of Ephesus (431)

Council of Chalcedon (451)

Great Schism (1054)

Michael Cærularius, ordered that all Latin (Catholic) churches in his see be closed. Pope Leo IX attempted to intercede, sending diplomats and a letter proclaiming the ultimate authority of the Roman see (based partly on the "Donation of Constantine," a forgery then thought to prove that Constantine empowered the Roman see over others). Cærularius ignored it, each side excommunicated the other and, while half-hearted attempts were made to reconcile, these fell apart—Christian unity was an unattainable ideal before the Crusades even started.

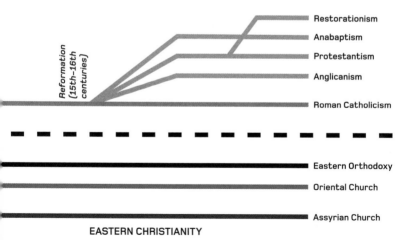

Restorationism

Anabaptism

Protestantism

Anglicanism

Reformation
(15th–16th
centuries)

Roman Catholicism

Eastern Orthodoxy

Oriental Church

Assyrian Church

EASTERN CHRISTIANITY

Inca

During the first millennium AD, western South America gave rise to many cultures including the Moche, Wari, and Tiwanaku empires (which used llamas as beasts of burden and sources of wool, and had extensive roads). Each in turn declined, perhaps due to climate. Around the 12th century, the Inca of Peru developed a small kingdom with Cusco as its capital. Under Pachacuti (r. 1438–71) and after, it became the largest empire in South America, ranging from the Pacific to the Amazon: Machu Picchu was constructed in this era.

Unlike northern Mesoamerican civilizations, the Inca had no writing, though they did use *quipus*—an intricate system of knotted cords—for numerical record keeping; along with well-kept roads, resettlement, and central storage, this helped keep the empire together under semidivine rulers (of various religions). In the early 1500s, the first trace of the Conquistadors arrived, in the form of smallpox. The eastern Amazon tribes remained disunited until well into colonial times.

Viracocha; Octabo Yngaɪ

The Crusades

Derived from the Latin word for a cross, "crusade" is the collective name for a series of religious conflicts from the 11th to the 14th century, most of which revolved around attempts by Europeans to "liberate" Jerusalem. The city had been captured from the Byzantine (Eastern Roman) empire soon after Muhammad's death, but as a holy site in Islam, too, the various caliphates—the Egyptian Fatimids and the Persian Seljuqs (or Turks)—had been fighting for control over it.

In 1095, the weakened Fatimids held Jerusalem, while the Turks had taken over Asia Minor. Byzantium's ruler Alexios I asked for Western help in defending the Eastern churches, whereupon Pope Urban II declared the First Crusade. The initial effort was a shambolic failure—huge crowds of peasants and minor nobles set off under the leadership of a priest called Peter the Hermit, with many thousands dying along the route and the starving mob raiding towns and farms along the way before an ignominious defeat at the hands of Turkish archers.

Reinforcements (including many aristocrats on the make) made it to Constantinople (where they were a problem for Alexios), crossed to Asia Minor and slowly made their way down the coast to Israel, capturing Jerusalem in 1099. Crusader kingdoms were carved out of the new conquests—the first of these to fall, Edessa, inspired the Second Crusade of 1145, which accomplished nothing for the Christians but became a *jihad* or holy war for Muslims.

In 1187, the Egyptian ruler Saladin, who had overthrown the weakened Fatimids, retook Jerusalem, triggering the Third Crusade (the famous one, with Richard I). Jerusalem remained very much in Muslim hands, but much of the rest of the surrounding Holy Land was recaptured for the Christians. A Fourth Crusade set out to conquer the Holy City but never even reached Israel, sacking Constantinople instead in 1204, and cementing the Schism. Crusading would continue for the rest of the century, but men and territory attenuated. The last important crusader outpost, Acre, was a useful port for the Silk Road: it fell to the Mamluks in 1291. Meanwhile, popes began declaring crusades elsewhere with varying success— the French Albigensian Crusade of 1209–29 stamped out the Cathar heresy of the Languedoc region with infamous brutality.

Genghis Khan and the Mongols

Temujin, born around 1162, was the third son of a Mongol chieftain, subjugated as a boy and forced to spend his youth as a prisoner of his father's former colleagues (the Tayichi'ud). He escaped and built a reputation as a fearsome raider, and in each campaign he offered conquered tribes a chance to join him. Defeating his former mentor, Toghrul, and former blood-brother, Jamukha, by 1206 Temujin was overall leader ("Genghis Khan") of the nomadic tribes collectively known as Mongols. Over the next 20 years he invaded northern China, swept through Persia to the Caspian Sea, then returned to China again—during which final campaign he died in 1227.

The Temujid empire expanded under his descendants from Indochina to Austria, halted only at the Battle of Ain Jalut in modern-day Israel (Crusader territory in 1260, but they gladly allowed a Mamluk army to defeat their common foe—the Mongols also had plans for Egypt). Kublai Khan, Temujin's grandson, established China's Yuan dynasty in 1271.

Magna Carta

Richard the Lionheart was not an outstanding English king —he seldom visited the country, was thwarted in the Third Crusade, and demanded huge sums from his subjects (a ransom of 150,000 marks when he was captured, plus money for wars in his native France). Nevertheless, Richard was rarely present to tax the English directly, so he was more fondly regarded than his brother John. Actual rebellion didn't break out until after Richard's death, with a combination of disasters. The Normandy possessions (William the Conqueror's original lands) broke away, a dispute about selection of a new Archbishop of Canterbury led to King John's excommunication, and the aristocracy rose up against him.

Magna Carta, signed in 1215 at Runnymede, was the first attempt to legally limit a king's powers. John shrewdly acceded to clearly defined responsibilities, but the charter was more important as a symbol to future generations than as an actual instrument—the rebellion dragged on until after John's death.

Mamluks

Haroun al-Rashid's son Mutasim made a practice of buying slaves and training them as faithful bodyguards, and as their power fragmented, the Abbasid caliphate soon came to depend on this military caste. They proved untrustworthy, however, and increasingly came to direct Abbasid power. Turkish Mamluk ibn Tulun briefly gained autonomy for Egypt in the ninth century, and after the Fatimids (who lost territory to the Crusaders) and the Ayyubids (who gained much of it back again), a Mamluk dynasty, the Bahri, finally took control in 1250.

The Crusaders were greatly weakened, and the Bahri moved eastward with ease after the Mongols obliterated the Abbasid seat of Baghdad in 1258. The Bahri created an empire of their own (halting the Mongol advance in 1260). The Burji displaced them in 1382, controlling Egypt and the Near East until Ottoman conquest in 1517. Even then, the Mamluks clung on, later mustering opposition to Napoleon in Egypt. Ottoman general Muhammad Ali massacred the last of them in 1811.

Ottoman empire

Like the Huns, to whom they were perhaps related, the Turks were nomadic, warfaring tribes from Central Asia (perhaps Chinese in origin—they are mentioned in early writings about the Silk Road). Under the leadership of their clan chieftain Seljuq (died *c.* 1038), one branch, the Oghuz, settled in Anatolia and adopted Islam in the 11th century. His grandson Tughril (*c.*990–1063) founded the Seljuq dynasty—expanding his influence as far as Baghdad, he established himself as protector to the fading Abbasid caliphs (in reality, the power behind the throne), and was rewarded with the title *sultan*. However, political dissent meant that considerable division had occurred by the time the Crusaders arrived, and the Mongols conquered even the surviving sultanate in Anatolia.

Another Oghuz warlord, Osman I (*c.*1258–1326), went in the other direction and carved out a kingdom from Byzantine territory, founding a dynasty that lasted until the 20th century, when it was finally overthrown by Kemal Atatürk. By the end of the century it had besieged Constantinople, but attacks by Tamburlaine, culminating in the 1402 Battle of Ankara, threw everything into chaos for a few years. Following the death of Sultan Bayezid I, his sons fought a bitter civil war until Mehmed I took control. The 1453 Fall of Constantinople gave the empire a new capital. For the next two centuries the empire expanded widely—European victory at the Battle of Lepanto put an end to its control of the Mediterranean but not Ottoman incursions into Europe. They took control of the Islamic Near East, including Egypt, and controlled the Silk Road. The *millet* system allowed different religious groups a certain autonomy in their legal affairs.

A slow decline began when Catherine the Great wrested the Crimea from Ottoman control, and Greek Independence revealed a fundamental weakness. The economy of the empire relied on continued expansion and, once this stopped, collapse was only arrested by periodic border skirmishes with other expanding empires (notably Russia and Austria-Hungary). European visitors to Constantinople noted the beggars and lassitude, even during the Crimean War. A final flourish at Gallipoli (1915–16) was insufficient to prevent the empire's ultimate collapse.

Tamburlaine

Mongol-descended settlers in Transoxania (Uzbekistan) became part-Turkic and Muslim. Timur, son of a local leader, was captured by Mongols and brought to Samarkand in the 1340s. Installed as a proxy leader, he proved intractable; thereafter, he became a mercenary, sustaining injuries that led to his epithet "Timur the Lame." His campaign of conquest was a mix of scholarship, propaganda, tactical genius, and unmitigated savagery. Unable to claim descent from Genghis Khan, he ruled through puppets: conquests included Moscow, Aleppo, Baghdad, Kashgar, and Delhi, bringing Islam to India. Some estimates claim 17 million casualties; he leveled entire cities and built pyramids of skulls as a deterrent. Yet he was also a scholar, corresponding with French and Castilian kings. His conquest of Ottoman-held Ankara made him a potential ally for some Christians, although he virtually wiped out the Nestorian sect. He met his end in 1405 while assailing Ming China amid unprecedently harsh winter and plague, though the Mughals were his dynastic descendants.

The Bibi Khanym mosque in Samarkand was constructed by Timur after his Indian campaigns of 1399.

Ming

China's Ming dynasty (1368–1644) emerged after the collapse of the Yuan dynasty (which had been founded by Kublai Khan, grandson of Genghis Khan) and slowly rebuilt China as an independent state. The Mongols continued harassing the new regime (at one point capturing the emperor, in the Tumu crisis), leading to the repair and rebuilding of the Great Wall. A new capital was created, at Beijing, in 1403. Literature and the arts had a high period, and Ming ceramics are greatly prized.

Famines caused by the Little Ice Age and economic troubles led to discontent. As European trade had led to an influx of silver, the dynasty had switched to a silver currency, instead of the Yuan paper money or the Song copper and iron coinage. When Spain introduced harsher protections, silver imports ceased— but taxes were paid in silver, rendering them unaffordable for many. The rebel Li Zicheng took Beijing and declared himself emperor in 1644, before being defeated in battle himself—the following dynasty, the Qing, ruled until 1911.

Hundred Years' War

A war that began with knights in armor ended with cannons, pistols, and year-round campaigning. Warfare altered more in this single long conflict than it had during the previous three millennia. England's Henry II had judiciously married Eleanor of Aquitaine and ruled over three-fifths of France, though his son John lost most of it (hence Magna Carta). Edward III pursued his claim to the French throne in 1337: a 1340 naval battle off Sluys destroyed the French fleet, ensuring English control of the Channel for 30 years. Edward and his son the Black Prince triumphed at the 1346 battle of Crècy, then took the port of Calais. Poitiers in 1356 was even more successful, with the capture of France's King John II.

With both sides financially exhausted and France facing peasant rebellion, truce was declared in 1360. A decade later, France's Charles V began quietly recapturing territory. He died in 1380, and his son, Charles VI, soon showed signs of madness. Various parties maneuvered for power and advantage at the court of the incapacitated king, with outright civil war erupting in 1407. Amid the turmoil, England's Henry V re-entered the war in 1415 with Burgundian support, overcoming a vastly larger French force at Agincourt (while the victory was due to skilled longbowmen, the first English casualty of a bullet fell here). His gamble had been to fight in October, after harvest and the fighting "season." Henry regained Normandy, married Charles the Mad's daughter Catherine, and was named heir to the French throne, supplanting Charles's son the Dauphin. However, Henry died in 1422.

In 1429, a peasant girl, Jeanne d'Arc, presented herself to the Dauphin, claiming that God had sent her to save France. She went to Orléans, where French soldiers believed her, lifting a siege days later (the Burgundians had withdrawn, leaving an outnumbered English army). Her leadership at Patay revealed weaknesses in English tactics, and her death at the stake in 1430 only enhanced her legend. The Dauphin (crowned Charles VII at Rheims) developed an artillery corps capable of defeating the longbow. Victories for the French came apace; Burgundy switched sides in 1435, and after the 1453 Battle of Castillon all English continental holdings were lost, barring Calais. Anglo-French tensions would continue until the Crimean War.

Black Death

Though far from the only plague in history, the pandemic that killed about one-third of Europe's population in four years from 1347 (and similar proportions elsewhere) is surely the best known. It spread on the Silk Road; Italian traders brought it from the Crimea (where it may have been carried by Mongols). The original vectors were fleas on black rats, but it may also have been passed by breathing. Famines added to the problem.

Many blamed witches or Jews but others, notably in France, believed people had brought this upon themselves through sin. In the aftermath, art depicting skeletons became common. In Britain, trade guilds (disproportionately spared thanks to their private water supplies) performed Bible stories as thanksgiving: "Mystery Plays" that gave rise to commercial theater. With labor in short supply and food relatively cheap, true feudalism became untenable, and wages began to be paid directly. Some invested this income in land and consolidated earnings into more land and trade, upsetting centuries of aristocratic privilege.

Habsburgs

German count Rudolf of Habsburg established his family's power with his election as "King of the Romans" (in effect, King of Germany) in 1273, and his subsequent acquisition of Austria, which became the family seat of power. By 1440, they were powerful enough for the Papacy to declare Frederick III Holy Roman Emperor, the first of two Habsburgs so honored. Second was Charles V, crowned in 1519, by which time the family had dynastic links across the continent. Frederick's son Maximilian married his son, Philip the Handsome, into Spain's royal house, and his granddaughter married the Hungarian heir, creating Austria-Hungary. Charles V ruled over the German possessions, Spain in the period of Conquistador expansion, and sporadically over the Netherlands, although this proved unwieldy and the dynasty split into Spanish and Austrian lines. Family inbreeding led to physical and mental problems such as the "Habsburg chin," and contributed to the extinction of both main lines, although cadet branches survived. Habsburgs continued to rule Austria until the Austrian Republic of 1918.

Wars of the Roses

Henry VI of England became king in infancy in 1422, but proved to be mentally unstable. His uncles ran a regency government, but split into factions over the Hundred Years' War, which England was losing. When Henry suffered a breakdown in 1453, the popular Richard of York (a successful war leader with a hereditary claim on the throne) became Lord Protector. Henry's wife Margaret of Anjou, exploiting the "peace party," banished Richard from court in 1455 after Henry recovered. Civil war followed, and parliament appointed Richard heir in 1460. Margaret fought on, killing Richard at the Battle of Wakefield, but her Lancastrian army was wiped out in 1461 at Towton, the most savage battle on English soil. Richard's eldest son, crowned Edward IV, crushed further rebellions including Margaret's last-ditch attack in 1471. Edward died in 1483, and his brother became King Richard III after the convenient disappearance of his young nephews. Welsh-born Lancastrian Henry Tudor finally defeated Richard at the 1485 Battle of Bosworth, and married Elizabeth of York to end the conflict.

Printing

Woodcuts had provided a means of reproducing images for a century in Europe before, *c*.1454, Johannes von Gutenberg adapted cider presses to print text using movable lead type. Chinese printing employed hardwood templates for individual pictograms, and water-based ink—Gutenberg adapted new oil paints from the Netherlands, allowing lower-quality paper to be used. Book ownership had hitherto been a sign of privilege, and the ability to read mainly a preserve of priests. Books were intensively worked, handmade artefacts—acts of devotion in themselves, often decorated (as with the Lindisfarne Gospels), and with the text corrupted slightly with each copy. Printed books were the start of Mass Production—Paris and Venice adapted the techniques, developing their own lettering ("Roman" and "Italic" respectively).

Literacy became a significant tool for followers of Martin Luther, who published Bibles in local languages. Inexpensive, identical texts enabled schooling to develop; individual tuition had been reserved for aristocratic families but the sons of merchants could be educated in bulk. With ready access to copies of influential texts, trade in books (and attempts to suppress them) went hand in hand with the Reformation and growth in capitalism. Governments and rebels alike took advantage of the new technology to circulate propaganda.

Arguably, the conception of the modern nation-state began to develop in earnest only after 1500, once significant numbers of books in indigenous languages had become available. While Humanist scholars such as Petrarch and Erasmus were international figures through Latin versions of their work, vernacular works (such as Boccaccio's *Decameron* and Chaucer's *Canterbury Tales*) had hitherto been personal or intended for performance—topical in every sense of the word. Mass-produced books were intentionally enduring and national. The ad hoc phonetic spellings of regional accents became codified, as written languages became the defining features of European nations. The products of each language were exportable, but increasingly a nation's culture was a private conversation. Self-determination and individual conscience formed the ideal for the next five centuries—a model that extended around the whole world after the Enlightenment.

The Medici

One of the most successful families in Renaissance Italy, the Medici first rose to prominence through the bank they established in 1397. Opening branches across the continent, they provided courts with funds and prefigured the type of international commerce now taken for granted. Cosimo de' Medici shifted the family's attention to politics (his neglect of the bank led to its collapse in 1494). He and his descendants effectively ran Florence, becoming hereditary rulers in 1530. As patrons of arts and sciences, they encouraged Michelangelo, Leonardo da Vinci, and Galileo among many others, while clever politicking saw them marry into European royal houses such as France's House of Bourbon and the Austrian Habsburgs. Several sons became popes. Leo X beautified Rome and ordered a printing press, with funds raised by selling the "indulgences" Martin Luther abhorred. Clement VII refused Henry VIII of England a divorce and allied the Papal States against the Habsburg Charles V—the resulting sack of Rome in 1527 ended their Renaissance patronage. The main line was extinct by 1737.

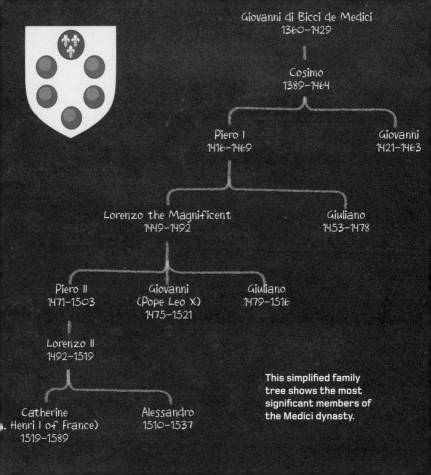

Giovanni di Bicci de Medici
1360–1429

Cosimo
1389–1464

Piero I
1416–1469

Giovanni
1421–1463

Lorenzo the Magnificent
1449–1492

Giuliano
1453–1478

Piero II
1471–1503

Giovanni
(Pope Leo X)
1475–1521

Giuliano
1479–1516

Lorenzo II
1492–1519

Catherine
. Henri I of France)
1519–1589

Alessandro
1510–1537

This simplified family
tree shows the most
significant members of
the Medici dynasty.

Fall of Constantinople

The vestigial Roman empire collapsed when the Ottomans invaded and captured its last independent capital in 1453. This was not the first time it had been taken—Crusaders had looted its wealth in 1204—but this time it was for good. Constantinople, reduced to essentially a city-state by this time, was still significant as a trading post on the land route into Asia. With this remnant of the Silk Road lost, Western powers began looking for maritime routes to the Indies, while Venice cheerfully took control of Mediterranean trade.

The Pope proposed a crusade; no one came. Religious zeal would combine with geopolitical motives in other ways after the Reformation. Until their failure to take Vienna in 1529, the Ottomans would make steady advances (into Hungary on the one side, attacks in Persia on the other) and France would even assist with attacks against the Habsburgs. Constantinople, renamed Istanbul, became the legal and cultural capital of the Ottoman empire, until that, too, fell in 1923.

Navigation

With the fall of Constantinople allowing the Ottomans to tax trade using the Silk Road, and use of the compass spreading from China, sea routes became more attractive for Europeans in the 15th century. Portuguese Prince Henry the Navigator (1394–1460) commissioned maps and trading expeditions around Africa, instigating a lucrative African slave trade. Portugal and Spain signed the 1479 Treaty of Alcáçovas dividing the world along an arbitrary meridian: Spain claimed territories to the west, Portugal those to the east. Portugal's objectives were the sources of spices and silk in China and the "Indies." Vasco da Gama reached India via South Africa in 1490, and trade routes were soon established. Ferdinand and Isabella of Spain sponsored an attempt to circumvent the Portuguese monopoly by a westward route; instead Columbus's 1492 voyage found lands unmentioned by Greek and Roman authorities.

England's John Cabot went in search of a Northwest Passage to the Indies (not sailed until 1906), reaching Newfoundland in

1497. He received a reward of £5 for discovering new fisheries. The Vikings had visited before, but the New World's potential as territory untouched by trade or rival powers now became clear. Spain continued sending expeditions west—Vasco de Balboa reached the Pacific in 1513, and Ferdinand Magellan organized a 1519–22 expedition that circumnavigated the globe. Only one of five ships returned, laden with valuable spices.

Spanish Conquistadors plundered the New World (Portugal took Brazil in defiance of treaties), while English settlers landed in what became the Thirteen States, with Dutch and French arrivals nearby. French fur trappers made North America a battleground in the Seven Years' War, but initially Anglo-Dutch rivalry was most important. Elizabeth I chartered the East India Company in 1600 (with disastrous repercussions for India). Holland's rival VOC hired Henry Hudson for its American ventures; he mapped the bay and river bearing his name, and Holland settled a strategic port at New Amsterdam.

In the 18th century, Britain made two final major breakthroughs for global navigation: James Cook proved that fruit prevented scurvy (a disease common on long sea voyagers), while John Harrison invented a reliable clock to ascertain longitude.

Ferdinand and Isabella

Roman Iberia (Spain and Portugal) was lost to Visigoths from AD 409, who in turn lost most of it to the Umayyad Muslims. From the tenth century, Christian warlords attempted to "purge" the peninsula from the north, while the southern Conviviencia waned as a new Islamic regime arrived to "purify" the lax customs of the Muslims there. Some fled north, preferring to live under the Reconquista in Castile, Aragon, or Navarre. The spread of Arabic knowledge into Europe accelerated as a result, including that of navigational equipment and charts.

In 1474, Ferdinand II of Aragon married Isabella I of Castile. By 1492, they had conquered the southern kingdom of Granada, and Spain as we know it came into being. After the monarchs signed a warrant ordering the forced conversion or expulsion of all Jews, many fled to Venice, benefiting that city enormously. Any who stayed faced the Inquisition. A confident Spain made dynastic marriages with Habsburgs and Tudors, and financed expeditions to compete with Portugal's Henry the Navigator.

Columbus granted an audience before Ferdinand and Isabella.

Safavid Persia

After a century's rule by descendants of Tamburlaine, Persia was conquered by a teenager in 1501. Isma'il was leader of the Safavids, an Islamic order once exiled to Uzbekistan, that had begun as Sufi but was by now Twelver Shi'ite. This amplified Persian emnity toward the Ottomans, and war erupted; Persia lost Iraq in 1555, and with the support of Azerbaijani Qizilbash warriors, Isma'il captured the capital of Tabriz.

His most eminent successor, Abbas, built a magnificent new capital at Isfahan, whose broad ethnic mix made it a nexus of trade: new crafts such as rugmaking were developed. European emissaries came here to circumvent Constantinople: two English soldiers, the Sherley brothers, reorganized Abbas's armies, but the Dutch VOC received preferential trading agreements, with Portuguese bases uprooted in 1602 and England's navy repelled a decade later. After an Afghan uprising in 1639, the power of the empire waned—once a Mughal force took Kandahar, its borders became those of modern-day Iran.

Conquistadors

In 1492, Christopher Columbus established a fort on the island of Hispaniola (now Haiti and the Dominican Republic), bringing back inhabitants as slaves for Ferdinand and Isabella. His fellow Italian voyager Amerigo Vespucci realized these were not the East Indies but unknown new lands. Hernán Cortés arrived in Mexico in 1520, bringing horses which, combined with the relative pallor of the Spanish, made them resemble Aztec deities. By the time the truth emerged, Spanish colonization was underway, killing many through disease and mistreatment.

Native alliances and the kidnap of Moctezuma II helped Cortés overthrow the Aztec empire. His cousin Pizarro took the Incan empire in 1533 (see Tupac Amaru). Both proved rich in precious metals that were exported to Spain, but increasing the money supply but not goods caused hyperinflation and ruined Spanish commerce. It also encouraged pirates and privateers (mostly English). Portugal, preoccupied in the east, still colonized Brazil, populating sugar and coffee plantations with African slaves.

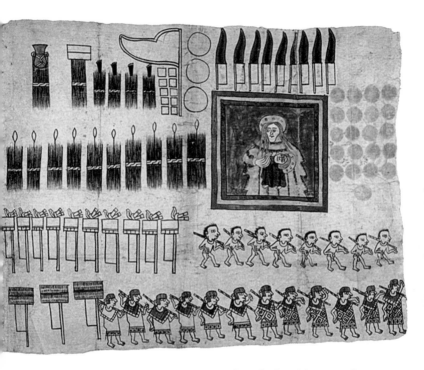

The Huexotzinco Codex, dating to shortly after the Spanish conquest,
includes one of the earliest Mesoamerican depictions of the Virgin Mary.

Martin Luther

Born Hans Luder in Saxony in 1483, Luther began as a keen Catholic monk at a time when, thanks to the Medici and Borgia popes, worldliness was the order of the day. Appalled by corruption, he devised a doctrine of redemption through faith rather than good works (such as donations to the church). In addition to tithes (donations of one-tenth of income), Catholicism was financed by selling of indulgences (remission of sins) for money. Luther wrote his *Ninety-Five Theses* against these practices in 1517, and further pamphlets and the printing press spread his "Protestant" ideas rapidly across Europe.

Pope Leo X demanded Luther recant at the Diet of Worms, and excommunicated him in 1521. Free of his vows, Luther translated a vernacular Bible and married. Other reformers—notably Calvin, Zwingli, and Knox—developed Protestant theologies of their own. England's Henry VIII found the Reformation politically expedient, while Holy Roman Emperor Charles V's defense of Catholicism pushed many German nobles into Protestantism.

Mughals

The Mughal dynasty produced 17 emperors, who from 1526 to 1707 subjugated and unified the Indian subcontinent, creating the richest court on Earth. Babar, lord of Ferghana and one of many princelings descended from Tamburlaine and Genghis Khan, was raised in Uzbekistan and the Safavid empire. He claimed Afghanistan and northern India in the last four years of his life, leaving it to Humayan in 1530. Deposed in 1540, he returned 15 years later, expanding his territory, and bringing with him artists and scholars from his Persian exile.

Akbar "the Great" ruled from 1556 and made major conquests in Hindu lands. He established a cult of personality, and allowed religious freedom in a notionally Muslim kingdom. Jehangir succeeded him in 1605, and Shah Jehan ruled 1627–58; grief at his wife's death led him to build the Taj Mahal (one of many distinctively Mughal monuments), but allowed his ambitious son Aurangzeb to depose and imprison him. Despite rising religious violence, Aurangzeb's reign marked the zenith of Mughal rule.

Reformation in England

Henry VII married off his heir Arthur, to Catherine of Aragon, Infanta of Spain, but his dynastic plans faltered with Arthur's death. His younger son, Henry, was being groomed as a future archbishop but, on becoming Henry VIII, was granted papal dispensation to wed his brother's widow. After years of marriage with only a single daughter, he sought to have the possibly blasphemous union annulled, but a new pope refused. Under the influence of advisors swayed by Luther, Henry founded a breakaway Church of England in 1536: he executed Lord Chancellor Thomas More for criticizing his expediency, but paradoxically continued to take Catholic Mass until his death.

Plundering monastic property boosted royal income, while former monks became tutors in schools for a rising bourgeoisie. Henry and Katherine's daughter, Mary I, returned England to Catholicism, burning 300 "martyrs" in a three-year reign; Henry's daughter by his second marriage, Elizabeth I, undid this, and England has remained at least nominally Protestant ever since.

Battle of Lepanto

The steady Ottoman advance since the Fall of Constantinople was finally halted in 1571. Pope Pius V called for a League of Christian countries to oppose the Turkish empire, specifically to relieve a siege in Cyprus. Don John of Austria commanded the fleet, with Spanish and Italian forces at the forefront (Protestant England declined, and France was embroiled in internal conflict). Lepanto was a small town at the narrowest part of the Gulf of Corinth (which divides Greece nearly in half near Thermopylae), and therefore a strategic point that had seen many owners—Venice had lost it to the Ottomans in 1499.

It was here that the League caught the main Ottoman fleet on October 7, 1571. Despite an Ottoman numerical advantage, Islamic casualties were about 30,000 while those of the Holy League were about 7,500 (and about as many Christian slaves as were liberated). The bulk of the Turkish naval command were killed and their composite bowmen were outgunned: archery would never decide another naval battle.

Nova of 1572

A synthesis of Christianity and Aristotelianism prevalent in Europe made sense to most people. Everything above the Moon was perfect and incorruptible, but mankind's sin made the Earth prone to decay, illness, and death. Planets moved in perfect circles around it, and were encased in spheres of adamantine. Nothing could change in the heavens.

Then, after an 8,000-year journey, light from a distant stellar explosion in Cassiopeia reached Earth in November 1572. The Renaissance mindset, with direct observation replacing learned assumptions from garbled classical authorities, was better prepared to accept such developments, but this new star or "nova," visible in daylight, was profoundly shocking: it coincided with increasing religious violence and fear of social upheaval. Danish astronomer Tycho Brahe's detailed studies proved that the nova was much further away than the Moon, and later provided the basis for a complete overhaul of ideas about the nature of the Universe.

Tycho Brahe's map depicting the "new star" of 1572.

Tupac Amaru

Following the Sapa Inca's death from smallpox, civil war between two of his sons had weakened the Incan empire before Spanish Conquistador Francisco Pizarro arrived in 1532. Inspired by his cousin Cortés' attacks in Mesoamerica, he had scouted the area in 1524, discovered the Incas had the art of smelting precious metal, and eventually persuaded Habsburg King Charles V to provide men to conquer the new lands.

Pizarro efficiently deployed his guns and cavalry in the Battle of Cajamarca, preserving his small force and kidnapping the emperor Atahualpa. He demanded and received a hefty ransom, then murdered the emperor and took Cusco in the confusion. Rebellions and puppet rulers followed, and Pizarro was killed by envious fellow Spaniards in 1541; the last of the Inca dynasty, Tupac Amaru launched a final offensive in 1572 and was consequently executed. Spanish control was firmly established, utilizing one particular Inca tradition that required the people to work a set number of days to support state mining.

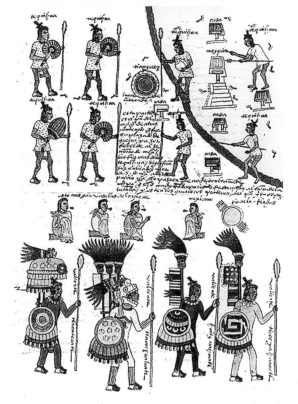

Intended for the eyes of the Holy Roman Emperor Charles V, the Codex Mendoza includes detailed depictions of Aztec history and everyday life.

Missionaries

Christianity spread by word of mouth before Constantine; but the Romans enforced conversion. Assyrian converts reached China in the Han era, St. Cyril spread Orthodoxy to Russia, and after the Reformation both schools of Western Christianity competed for converts across the ever-expanding known world. Francis Xavier's Jesuit Order were Catholics, most active in China, Japan, and parts of South America under the Conquistadors. Many proselytized less the further they went from Rome and the longer they stayed: Matteo Ricci developed a dictionary and translated Euclid's *Elements* into Chinese in 1607. After the Sakuko Edict, attention switched to Indochina.

Protestant missions, mostly Anglican, were active in Britain's sphere of influence (though the USA sent some too). Often, these were the first Westerners to reach remote areas: David Livingstone established a mission in Uganda while seeking the source of the Nile. Stories of Old Testament freedom fighters inadvertently inspired 20th-century liberation movements.

Jesuit missionary Matteo Ricci alongside the bureaucrat and scholar Xu Guangqi, an early convert to Christianity and long-term colleague of Ricci.

Ivan the Terrible

Ivan IV (1530–84) was not the first Russian ruler to style himself Tsar (that was his grandfather Ivan III, who halted the Mongols). Like Louis XIV, his father died young, leaving him to be raised in among court intrigue. His conquests were extensive (Kazan, Astrakhan, Siberia—all previously held by the Golden Horde), yet a protracted attempt at Livonia failed and the Crimeans successfully raided Moscow in 1571. During his reign, English traders also penetrated to the northern port of Archangel, starting the Muscovy Trading Company.

Ivan's first and happiest marriage was to Anastasia Romanovna: after her death in 1560 (possibly to poison) he began to earn his sobriquet. He mistrusted the aristocratic *boyars*, harassing them with laws, forced resettlement, and massacres. He also started a secret police, the *oprichnikis*. Like his descendant Peter the Great, he killed his own son. His eventual heir, Feodor I, died without issue, ending the Rurikid dynasty—Romanovna's family went onto establish the House of Romanov.

Ulster Plantations

Queen Elizabeth I oversaw a cultural revival in England but, as a Protestant, was excommunicated by Pope Pius V in 1570. This allowed Catholic states to invade without fear, and Spain duly attempted a naval assault in 1588. The Armada was halted by English privateers and an unexpected hurricane, but threats remained. Catholic Ireland seemed a likely base for invasions: Elizabeth's father and sister had both been declared rulers of the island (the latter with Vatican consent), and her courtier Essex began a systematic colonization of Ulster (the northeast of Ireland) as though it were unoccupied. He viciously crushed opposition, but was himself executed by his monarch.

Elizabeth's successor, James VI of Scotland (James I of a unified Britain), accelerated the sporadic colonization by Scots Protestants, especially after a Catholic terror cell almost destroyed Parliament and himself in the infamous Gunpowder Plot. Many relocated for economic rather than ideological reasons, but by 1640 there were 40,000 Protestant settlers.

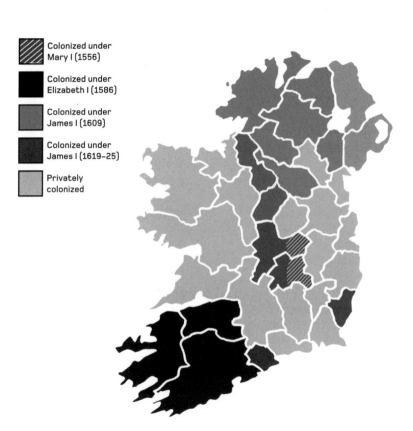

Colonized under
Mary I (1556)

Colonized under
Elizabeth I (1586)

Colonized under
James I (1609)

Colonized under
James I (1619–25)

Privately
colonized

Thirty Years' War

Several overlapping European conflicts are grouped together under the umbrella of the Thirty Years' War, encompassing the Reformation and its backlash, conflict between the Habsburgs and their rivals, and straightforward warfare between neighboring nations. The wars can be split into five phases, beginning in 1618 and ending in 1648; the first four lasted three to five years each. The initial conflict seems straightforward: the succession in Bohemia after the colorful Rudolph II (also Holy Roman Emperor) and his brother Matthias died without male heirs. Rudolph had increased religious tolerance in Bohemia, while his empire had lost land in Austria and Hungary to the Ottomans. Matthias deposed him but died soon after. Bohemia was ripe for reconversion as part of the Counter-Reformation: a Catholic claimant, Ferdinand, and a Protestant, Frederick, gained support split mainly on religious lines. A revolt, erupting after two Catholic regents were hurled from a third-floor window (the "Defenestration of Prague"), put Frederick on the Bohemian throne while Ferdinand became

Holy Roman Emperor. Ferdinand's Habsburg backers attacked Frederick's lands in the Palatinate (around the Rhine), and Phase Two began when the Dutch, seeking independence from the Spanish Habsburgs, came to Frederick's aid.

By 1625, Habsburg victories in the Rhine triggered an alliance between Catholic France, Lutheran Denmark, Britain (whose King James I was Frederick's father-in-law), and the Dutch. The Holy Roman empire was aided by a Bohemian named Wallenstein, whom nobody trusted—the allies had him removed. In 1630, King Gustavus Adolphus of Sweden intervened to claim German lands and prevent Habsburg dominance: only France supported him (and mainly financially). The empire struck back, recalling Wallenstein to repel the Swedes (the king died and his daughter Queen Christina was crowned aged six)—Emperor Ferdinand then had Wallenstein assassinated. From 1634, a Franco-Spanish conflict raged in Germany, allowing the Swedes to capture Bohemia. The Treaty of Westphalia finally brought the wars to an end, with Catholicism reimposed in Bohemia and Austria, Sweden paid to leave (but retaining northern German lands) and France holding Alsace. By Louis XIV's reign, France had become the dominant geopolitical power: future European wars would hinge on nationality rather than religion.

Dutch East India Company (VOC)

After gaining independence from Habsburg rule in 1609, the Netherlands rapidly expanded its commercial enterprises, soon outshining Venice. Following the model of England's East India Company, the Verenigde Oostindische Compagnie was a means of exploiting the vast appetite for luxury goods and medicinal herbs blocked by the Ottomans. Breaking Portugal's stranglehold on shipping routes to Southeast Asia, the Dutch traded directly with Japan: following the Anglo-Dutch War of 1667, a tiny nutmeg-producing island was worth exchanging for New Amsterdam (modern Manhattan). State coordination allowed each ship to maximize the worth of its cargo, and pioneered the shared-risk public issue of stocks. As voyages showed 400 percent profits, speculation was inevitable, even after salutary "bubbles" such as the disastrous "tulip mania." With their European neigbors distracted in religious wars, talent flowed to a new country with few aristocrats and powerless clergy. By the time the "Dutch golden age" faded, the habit of speculation was embedded in markets everywhere.

"Triangle Trade"

Slaves existed in the Americas before European contact, but these were generally only war captives, and their children were set free. Columbus acquired Native American slaves on his voyages for Ferdinand and Isabella, and Spanish Conquistadors tried using the local population for forced labor, resulting in horrifying mortality rates. Portugal already used African slaves on its Atlantic islands, so quickly expanded the system—40 percent of imported slaves (about 10 million; many more died en route, or fighting kidnappers in Africa) went to Brazil's plantations. Virginia's tobacco crop absorbed more labor than indentured English servants could provide, so those colonies adopted slavery, too. Eventually, trading patterns developed: ships left from England or Holland carrying trade goods to exchange in Africa for slaves; ships loaded with slaves would travel to the Americas; and raw materials such as sugar cane were in turn shipped to Europe to make into trade goods. New England traders joined in eventually, but ships would rarely sail the entire triangle.

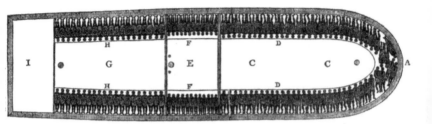

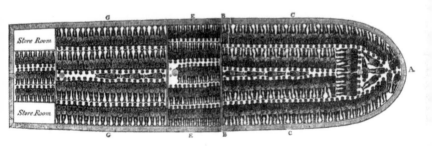

A contemporary illustration shows the typical packing of a slave ship,
with its human cargo shackled together and barely able to move
throughout the long sea voyage.

Puritanism

A form of Protestant fundamentalism originating in Zurich, Puritanism spread to Scotland (refined by John Calvin) and thence England. Its doctrinal radicalism and disproportionate influence reflect Millenarian beliefs in 17th-century Europe. Protestants considered intercession between the individual and God to be corrupting, and removed clergy, iconography, and ritual. Convinced the Day of Judgment was set for 1666, Puritans tolerated fewer concessions to "heretical" Catholicism than most Protestants. It spread through the Parliamentarian army in the English Civil Wars, and the execution of King Charles I seemed to conform to biblical prophecies.

One sect, the "Quakers," smoked enough tobacco to hallucinate and were considered a greater threat than Catholic terrorists. Another group left England when their demands were not met, and alienated even tolerant Amsterdam. Hiring the *Mayflower*, they crossed the Atlantic, interpreting their safe passage as sanction for imposing their will on the New World.

A cartoon from the era of the English Commonwealth satirizes puritan attempts to ban the celebration of Christmas.

Queen Christina

The only child of King Gustavas Adolphus, Christina was elevated to the throne of Sweden in 1632 at the age of six. Once of age, she moved to end the Thirty Years' War that had killed her father (though on less than satisfactory terms for Sweden). Emulating Rudolf II of Bohemia, she sought out artists, scientists, and scholars such as philosopher Rene Descartes. Ferocious curiosity led her to abandon the state religion, Lutheranism, for Catholicism, in which she also found flaws. This forced her abdication and replacement by Charles X.

The ex-queen cut her hair short, adopted male clothing, and traveled to southern Europe, collecting talented protégés and attempting to broker power: bravura plans included a scheme to become Queen of Naples and intercede between Spain and France. Governments took her seriously—she was influential, unpredictable, and formidably educated. She petitioned her friend Pope Clement X after Louis XIV withdrew the Edict of Nantes, and is one of just three women buried in the Vatican.

Coffee houses

The habit of drinking coffee and using coffee houses as meeting places began in Constantinople c.1475, and was spread by merchants. After Oliver Cromwell allowed Jews to return to England during the 1650s, coffee houses soon opened in Oxford and London: some 3,000 were in business under the Restoration monarchy of the 1660s, acting as centers of information, commerce, and dissent. The Stock Exchange, auction houses, and insurance brokers had their genesis here, as did newspapers and satirical pamphlets, party politics, the Bank of England, and the South Sea Bubble.

Ottoman-Habsburg wars left Vienna similarly enthused: adding cream and sugar, and associated pastries, began here. France caught on soon after, and the Enlightenment was arguably a result of this culture. Trade in beans and sugar altered the routes of the "Triangle Trade" and, paradoxically, led to coffee's displacement in Britain by a new fad, tea. Elsewhere, however, coffee remained popular.

Sakoku Edict

Europeans reached the Far East by sea by the 1500s, and missionaries and traders soon made friendly contact with Japan, at a time when the country was more outward-looking than hitherto. Shinto had some elements in common with Catholic ritual, but the concepts of Heaven and Hell ran athwart ancestral spirits as immanent forces. After Tokugawa Ieyasu successfully reunified the country with victory at the Battle of Sekigahara in 1600, he established a line that would stay in power until the 19th century. Mistrust of outside influences had led to persecution of Christians, but trade with Portuguese merchants continued until 1635, when Iemitsu issued the Sakoku Edict. This forbade Christianity and ended foreign trade except with the Dutch East India Company (VOC), who didn't proselytize. The policy persisted until 1858, when an American warfleet led by Commodore Perry led Japan to reopen its ports. Meanwhile, Jesuits remained welcome in China under Kangxi until 1715, when Pope Clement XI was persuaded that Catholicism could not accommodate Buddhism.

Emperor Iemitsu,
who proclaimed the
longstanding Sakoku edict.

Louis XIV

France's "Sun King" (1638–1715) reconfigured French state bureaucracy, built the hugely expensive palace of Versailles (where he held court among subservient aristocrats) and undertook several, mostly fruitful, wars. In his last and most disastrous, the War of the Spanish Succession, France went to war with the rest of Europe to place Louis's grandson Philip on the Spanish throne, after the Habsburg Charles II died heirless.

Louis inherited the throne at the tender age of four: a childhood spent in the shadow of the Fronde antimonarchist movement and the execution of his English counterpart Charles I did little to discourage his belief in the Divine Right of Kings. Neither did an extravagant private life and religious warfare across Europe temper his belligerent Catholicism. When he revoked the Edict of Nantes, created the previous century to stop the religious carnage, around 200,000 Protestants fled the country. State centralization also hampered French colonies before the Seven Years' War.

Peter the Great

The Russian empire had largely been forged by the time Peter I (1672–1725) came to the throne at the age of ten. Siberia had recently been conquered, but Russia remained feudal with no bourgeoisie or infrastructure. Famously, Peter traveled to the West incognito (in a delegation unsuccessfully advocating an anti-Ottoman alliance), hiring technical experts to help modernize his state, moving its focus westward.

St. Petersburg (a small Baltic port captured from Sweden) replaced Moscow as his capital. Aside from Persia (where the Treaty of Constantinople confirmed his territorial gains to the south), his major conflict was the Great Northern War with Sweden. Its king, Charles XII, was a brilliant military tactician but died in battle, cementing Russian control of the Baltic on sea and land. At home, Peter overhauled the taxation system and created a civil service. After executing his son Alexei Petrovich (fearing a conspiracy), he was succeeded by his wife Catherine, the first female ruler of Russia.

Newcomen's atmospheric engine

Although the ancient Greeks had invented various steam devices, these were mostly for show. Robert Boyle's 1662 work on the interrelated pressure, volume, and temperature of gases laid the groundwork for the first practical industrial application, developed around 1710. Thomas Newcomen's engine was a machine to pump water out of mines, reducing the risk of toxic, explosive methane released by damp coal.

Earlier designs had used the condensation of steam directly to move water; Newcomen's practical experience led him to design a rocking cradle in which a weight is lifted on a pivot by downward pressure of air on the other side as a chamber containing steam is cooled. Later models were sufficiently robust and predictable that they could operate with little maintenance. Newcomen's company sold hundreds of pumps across Europe over the next 50 years. The safer deep mining of coal in great quantities fueled the production of steel and allowed greater use of steam power in the century ahead.

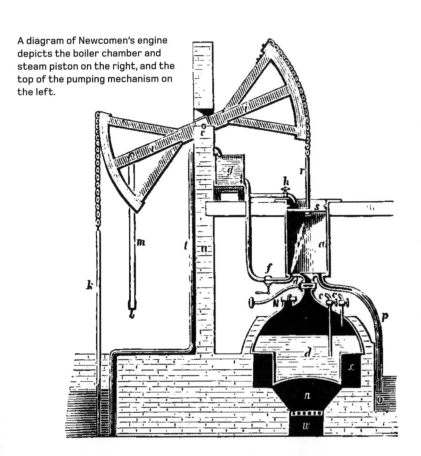

A diagram of Newcomen's engine depicts the boiler chamber and steam piston on the right, and the top of the pumping mechanism on the left.

Ashanti empire

The area constituting present-day Ghana has been inhabited since prehistory, but its main ethnic group, the Akan, seem to have moved there around the last millennium. Many local kingdoms were already engaged in trade when the Portuguese navigators arrived in the 15th century. Ghana is rich in minerals (hence the "Gold Coast"), and European powers all sought local favor, especially when the "Triangle Trade" began. Coastal Africans were well paid for providing inland African slaves.

The Ashanti kingdom became dominant in the 17th century under Osei Tutu, who established the Golden Stool as a symbol of power and began consolidation. The Ashanti developed a keen army, trained with guns, and capably opposed Western forces. Britain craved their wealth and, after several wars, finally forced the Ashanti to accept protectorate status in 1902. Ghana's independence in 1957 heralded a new relationship between African nations and former colonists (the "Wind of Change")—today, it is a prosperous constitutional democracy.

South Sea Bubble

The first stock-market inflation-and-crash cycle for which reliable data exist allows comparison between reality and the popular depiction. Founded in 1711 on the model of the East India Company, Britain's South Sea Company hoped to gain a monopoly of South American trade upon Spain's seemingly inevitable capitulation in a war. With the rise of an information network through the coffee houses, small investors confidently purchased shares—75 percent of the electorate owned shares by 1720 (12 percent of shareholders were women).

Laws to control more frivolous ventures boosted confidence in the Company. In the first nine years the dividend rose tenfold, but rumors of difficulties led to the peak price halving over August 1720. Latecomers lost fortunes: by December the share price was just 20 percent of June's level, but still slightly up on January. By then most had cut their losses, including writers who amplified the blip's notoriety. This archetypal bubble led to changes in British law and influenced the study of economics.

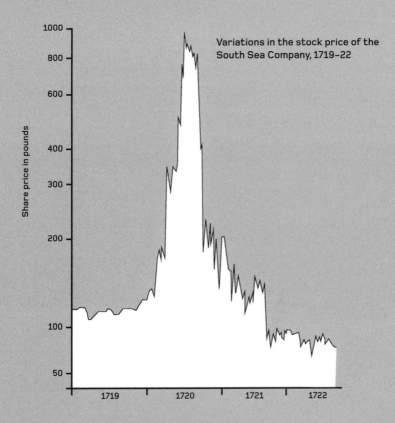

Variations in the stock price of the South Sea Company, 1719–22

Nadir Shah

Born into a peasant family in 1688, Nadir was sold into slavery by Uzbeks as a child. As a mercenary, he joined an Afghan army against them, until they stopped paying; the Afghans had conquered and humiliated the Safavid empire, so Nadir now joined them against the Afghans. Tamasp II became Persia's shah, but Nadir wielded the real power: he pursued the former invaders to Kabul and then India, defeating Mughal forces and taking Delhi. The captured Peacock Throne became a symbol of Persian power until the ayatollahs. In 1732, he deposed Tamasp, becoming shah in 1736 and returning Persia to Sunni Islam.

Nadir assaulted the Ottomans and Russia, formed a navy and captured Oman and Bahrain, using his army to enforce taxation. He grew increasingly paranoid (more so after attempts on his life), and was beheaded in 1747 by one of his own generals. The empire fell into factional disarray, and Afghanistan became a nation, while Europeans, alerted to Mughal vulnerability, exploited Maratha and Sikh efforts to fill the power vacuum.

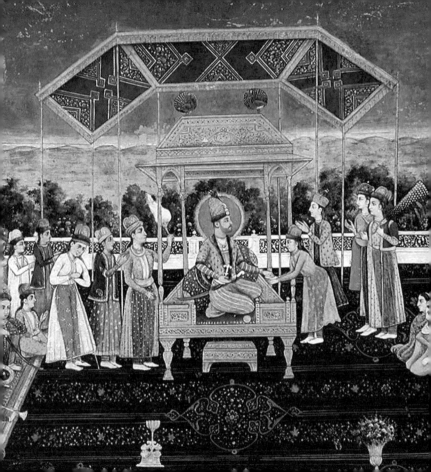

Treaty of Constantinople

One of Peter the Great's projects was to control the Black and Caspian seas, preventing the Ottoman empire from cutting off access to the Mediterranean. The controlling Persian dynasty was weak (Nadir Shah later took control after civil war), and the Russo–Persian War (1722–3) ended in Russian victory. The following year, the Ottomans agreed the Treaty of Constantinople, confirming Russia's gains.

In practical terms, it meant little: the 1732 Treaty of Resht gave many territories to Persia (with the Russians supporting it as a buffer against the Ottomans). Russia wouldn't launch another major Persian attack until the century's end. This represented Russia's first steps into the Middle East—Britain gained control of India after 1763, and the region became enmeshed in the "Great Game" of British–Russian geopolitics. Napoleon's rise to power complicated the situation: Britain, which favored Persia as a buffer between Russia and India, could not directly aid Russia's rivals while joining it in the anti-French alliance.

A map of the area around the Black Sea highlights the critical importance of regions such as the Crimea and the Ottoman-controlled city of Istanbul for Russian sea access.

Steel

An alloy of iron and carbon, steel had existed for millennia before Prague armorers developed a more efficient means of manufacture by slow addition of carbon. Sir Basil Brooke adapted this method when he introduced it to England c.1620. Large-scale ironworking was one of the main developments of Britain's Industrial Revolution in the late 18th century.

Charcoal was the traditional agent used to remove impurities from iron ore and add carbon, but with mining made economic by Newcomen, coke (refined coal) became available. It could be measured and graded minutely, making it possible to work with low-grade ores and construct entire bridges, railroad lines, and even ships. Sweden's better-quality ore, and the development of large crucibles in the 1740s, made steel-making competitive. With advances in chemistry, pure oxygen was identified as the means to expel excess carbon and silicon from molten iron. In 1855 Sir Henry Bessemer developed a giant cradle-like forge that sent jets of air through the smelt from below.

Bessemer converters like the ones shown here force air (later pure oxygen) through the molten iron from below, igniting and burning off impurities to produce a steel-grade metal.

Seven Years' War

The conflict of 1756–63 can be considered the first global war, fought as much in the colonies as between the official European combatants. During the War of the Austrian Succession (1740–48) Habsburg Maria Theresa had claimed the Austrian throne, but the rising German state of Prussia (under Frederick the Great) had seized the wealthy province of Silesia. Diplomatic shuffling resulted in Austria, Russia, and France at war with a British-funded Prussia.

The French had solid relations with the Native Americans, and allied with them in North America. A young general, George Washington, honed his guerrilla warfare tactics against them, and British colonists captured most of France's territories other than those granted to Spain. Much the same happened in India, where French colonies were lost. Back in Europe, however, Prussia was near collapse when the new German-born tsar, Peter III, withdrew Russian troops and arranged a peace treaty that left Europe's boundaries unchanged.

Catherine the Great

Tsaritsa of Russia from 1762 to 1796, Catherine II was an effective conqueror, ruler, and polymath. Born to a German dynasty in 1729, she was married to Peter III, who succeeded the immensely popular Elizabeth (Peter the Great's daughter, who had continued his reforms and nearly defeated Prussia in the Seven Years' War). Peter III, also German, made peace instead and was shortly assassinated. Thereafter Catherine took decisive control. Her husband had laid claim to Russian Orthodox church lands, and Catherine pursued this claim, as well as overhauling the morass of the Russian legal system. In wars with the Ottomans, Russia gained the Crimea, Black Sea ports, and the Ukraine. When Poland was partitioned (several times), she won another healthy chunk of territory for Russia.

Her court celebrated culture and French Enlightenment ideals. She promoted a new smallpox vaccine by taking it herself, corresponded with Voltaire, and wrote endlessly—satires, fairy tales, memoirs and, as she was dying, a history of Russia.

Lisbon earthquake

On November 1, 1755, the Portuguese city of Lisbon was laid waste by the devastating combined effects of an earthquake, tsunami, and fire. The event was arguably the first time that a government mounted the kind of rescue operations expected in a modern-day disaster (compared to spontaneous public responses and actions by insurance companies during the 1666 Great Fire of London). The Marquess of Pombal, who was in practical control of the government, called out the army to keep rioting to a minimum —there was firefighting, mass burial (at sea, to prevent plague), and careful scientific surveys and analysis in the aftermath.

The effect on Enlightenment Europe was considerable—the loss of life led to introspection. Voltaire wrote *Candide* to question whether this was "the best of all possible worlds." Kant interrupted his philosophy for the study of geology. Lisbon was rebuilt with quake-proof buildings, but the cost and loss brought an end to Portugal's phase of imperial expansion.

House of Saud

In 1744, Muhammad ibn Saud paired up with the orthodox Sunni leader Muhammad ibn Abd al-Wahhab to establish an independent theocracy in what is now Saudi Arabia (al-Wahhab's family remains allied with Saud's today, one handling politics, the other religion). It was theoretically part of the Ottoman empire (then at a low ebb after exhausting wars with Russia), but the Turks only retook the territory in 1818, and even then the Sauds quickly reestablished another state. A competing pro-Ottoman clan, the Al Rashids, forced them into exile in 1891, provoking considerable fighting; the British (and in particular Lawrence of Arabia), aiming to destabilize the Ottoman empire during World War I, aided the Sauds in defeating their rivals. King Abdulaziz unified Saudi Arabia, officially declaring it a kingdom in 1932. After large oil reserves were found in Iran and Bahrain, he entered into negotiations over rights, and Standard Oil began extraction in 1938. Oil wealth, and custody of the Islamic holy cities of Mecca (opposite) and Medina, made this family the lynchpin of the Arab world.

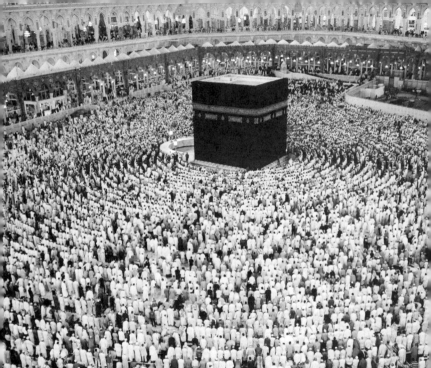

Enlightenment

This European movement had two poles: the exercise of reason over superstition, and exaltation and humility in the face of the Sublime—beauty, nature, and other absolutes. These tended in different directions: the former to reductionism, the latter toward Romanticism (a Platonic, antimaterialist artistic ideal). The movement originated in Paris, Edinburgh, and Weimar, spreading to London and New England. In many ways, the Enlightenment completed Renaissance Humanism, which ushered in, yet contradicted, the Lutheran Reformation.

System-building was a defining characteristic: Diderot's *Encyclopèdie*, condensing all knowledge into 28 volumes, was an early manifestation. Other key works include Rousseau's *Social Contract* and the US Declaration of Independence. Adam Smith, then Karl Marx and Sigmund Freud, attempted to apply scientific laws to human affairs. The Terror, Stalin's Purges, and the Holocaust have all been pinned on Enlightenment values, but so have Civil Rights, Abolitionism, and Universal Suffrage.

The frontispiece of *L'Encyclopèdie* shows an allegory of countless bounties, including scientific knowledge, descending from Truth.

Factories

For centuries, weaving had been a literal cottage industry, providing extra income for farmers and the elderly. By breaking the process into small, repetitive tasks that one person could do all day, Richard Arkwright and others developed the idea of purpose-built factories in 18th-century Britain. Arkwright provided weekly wages and enforced strict hours for his workers, but experienced weavers protested at machines destroying their livelihoods. His factories, based on rivers in northern England, used waterwheels to drive machines and produce fabrics on a large scale. Thanks to steam, however, power looms and other forms of mass production could soon be located wherever there was unskilled labor.

The new methods were a British trade secret until Samuel Slater defected to America in 1789. He founded the first US textile factories in Rhode Island; industry favored the North here also. The South, meanwhile, built its economy around cotton, with slaves supporting labor-intensive harvesting.

The Declaration of Independence

Anger over colonial taxes (alongside higher concerns over representation) inspired the Boston Tea Party of 1773, with repercussions that soon led to the Battles of Lexington and Concord. Boston came under siege, and war broke out in earnest. After a year of this, the Continental Congress, governing body of Britain's American colonies, decided independence was the only answer. Thirteen dependencies formally seceded in a document signed on July 2, 1776.

Thomas Jefferson's initial draft was amended in committee: English activist Thomas Paine's bestseller *Common Sense* had delineated arguments for independence to popular acclaim in both nations, even offering ideas for a permanent congress. The Articles of Confederation that served as a temporary constitution were designed to deal with current problems. The symbolic power of the document, denouncing remote rule and explicitly arguing for the right to create a nation-state, was huge: it served as model for dozens of other countries.

In CONGRESS. July 4, 1776.

The unanimous Declaration of the thirteen united States of America.

The Agrarian Revolution

By 1750, Britain's available agricultural land had increased, partly through Dutch drainage technology. After three centuries of "enclosures," farmland was concentrated in the hands of a few; farmers subscribed to journals that publicized concepts such as selective breeding and crop rotation, and the planting of clover, legumes, or root vegetables to refresh nitrogen in the soil. Potatoes became a staple, turnips a cash crop, and winter silage was stored in larger farmsteads. The average weight of livestock doubled between 1710 and 1795.

As the amount of agricultural labor required fell, the Industrial Revolution absorbed unskilled workers. Industrialization fed back into farming with new machinery and steel ploughs. By 1850, Britain's population was 16.6 million, with an unprecedentedly low 22 percent working on the land. As Britain became a dominant economic and military force, other nations applied these techniques, with generally beneficial short-term results (but see the Dust Bowl and Stalin).

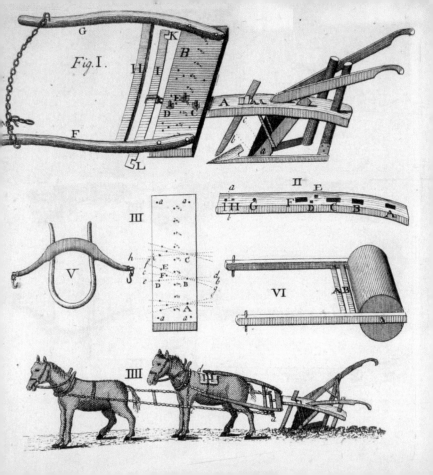

Cook and Australia

Australia has been inhabited for more than 40,000 years, and by the 18th century the Aboriginal population had reached a million, with hundreds of languages, sophisticated religious beliefs, and a painting tradition that survives today. In 1605, Dutch East Indies governor Willem Jansz had landed on the western coast without realizing he had found a continent.

British Captain James Cook (1728–79) led three voyages to the still-unexplored Pacific. His expeditions gathered copious scientific data—a stop in Tahiti introduced the Admiralty to breadfruit, prompting the *Bounty*'s famous voyage. Cook discovered that citrus fruit counteracted scurvy, making longer voyages viable. In 1770, he landed in the once-theoretical *Terra Australis*, mapping the coast and dubbing the location Botany Bay. Some 18 years later, with Virginia no longer available for convict settlement, Britain started the penal colony of Sydney at nearly the same spot. The indigenous population suffered horrendous mistreatment.

A CHART OF THE SOUTHERN HEMISPHERE;

shewing the Tracks of some of the most distinguished Navigators:

By Captain JAMES COOK, of his MAJESTY's Navy.

Tipu Sultan

Hyder Ali, commander-in-chief of the armies of Mysore in soutern India, and later its sultan, trained his first son to be either a scholar or a soldier. In 1767, aged 16, Tipu led his first army and captured the ruling family of Malabar. Hyder Ali's alliance with the French made him suspicious of the British, but after defeating them at Madras he extracted a treaty. In 1771, the East India Company delayed honoring its obligation to assist when Mysore was attacked by Maratha.

Now identifying the Company as his main enemy, Hyder began a second war (1780–84). He died in 1782; his heir Tipu pioneered the use of rockets as weapons, forcing a stalemate and the Treaty of Mangalore. However, a third war (1789–92), lacking outside assistance due to the French Revolution, ended with Tipu's sons as hostages and the Company gaining more ground than it had earlier lost. The fourth and final war faltered as the Mamluks undid Napoleon in Egypt. Rather than flee, Tipu stood and fought to the death at Seringapatam in May 1799.

A cartoon by British artist James Gilray satirizes the 1791 British retreat from Tipu's stronghold of Seringapatam.

Thailand

The kingdom of Ayutthaya, founded in the 14th century, adopted an isolationist outlook to Europe in the 17th century, but engaged in many regional wars. Burma seized and destroyed its capital in 1767. King Taksin reestablished the kingdom of Siam but was himself overthrown in 1782; army general Thong Duang established the (still extant) Chakri dynasty, ruling as Rama I and founding a new capital, Bangkok.

European powers increasingly controlled the Southeast Asian peninsula through the 19th century: the Chakri cautiously adopted Westernization where useful, courting Napoleon III and Victoria alike. Rama V (1853–1910) became famous for his reforms, including railroads and the abolition of slavery, and for a memoir by his English nanny. The Great Depression caused unrest that forced the monarchy to cede power; the military took control (renaming the country Thailand), remaining neutral in World War II until the Japanese invaded. Military dictatorships continued, but Thailand largely avoided the Indochina wars.

CHINE

LA   ROYAUME

Menan song   Pitchiou   Ras

Royaume   Mehon

D'ARACAN   Bengala Ropr

Chacingan   Dunqua Aracan Toron   Tatong   Pitchiou

Massaron   Debaca   AVA   Janqulouc   Lacouta   CACHO

Riv. d'Aracan   Lactora   Kaïn   Pithnolouck

I. Chedub   Yabta Polanga   Bor   Pitlam out   TUNQUIN

Santre Chalcu   Rakum   Peverdout   Lan-chang

Joura Ally   ou Silankout   Chaobun

ROYAUME DE   Mede   Pitchit   Quebo   GOLPHE

Ardou   PEOU   Casboch   DE

les Buffes   Pegu   Pegu   ROYAUME   Passou   TUNQUIN

Pronghu Pa   Knas   Campohape   Cuitai   Bede Pekin   D'HAINAN

Mero   Dongou   ROYAUME

I. Negraille   Cambori   Lacousesvan   Kehooa   I. Canton

Cap Ngrais   Sya   Tchunst   Quambis   Rolay

I. du Diamant   Bala   Martaban   DE   Boutra   Qui

La Nogada   Draga   Prahat   Baye de Touran   Cheano   Kiangrau

I. Priaparis   Louvo   SIAM   Boston   Haies

I. des Cocos   Tehnaat   Peravth   Bankim   Sombochut   Daubon

Narcodam   Blancasva   Leveck   Sombok   Cnaling

Grand Andaman   Pointe Tavaye   Cambya   Strponch   Gualing

Archipel de   Lisan   Logun   ROYAUME DE   Bandas

Petites   Iles Racos   Mergui   Corcena   Hollandois   CAMBOIE   Yunihin

I. Cin   Pionempena   Babanonh   Baye Comorin

du Andanson   I. Bardia   Way   Bata.   Pointe Paderon

I. Samcori   Chesponanne   Cap de Sable

Patanor   I. Carmon   Wai   I. de Gablas

Cernane   I. Cara

Logan   I. Papier   I. Payan   Isle Condor

Lesor   I. Losin   I. Ubi

Singor

CARTE   Patane   Pinaisa

DES ROYAUMES DE   R. Siri

SIAM   I. de

DE TUNQUIN   Junk Seilon   Cap Patane

Pegu, Ava Aracan &c   R. de Calaba   I. Losin

Echelle de Lieues Communes   Roman   M   Redaor

25   5   7   Nord de l'Isle   A   L

de Sumatra   A   Longitude du Meridien de Paris

GOLPHE   DE   SIAM

GOLPHE   DE   TUNQUIN

ROYAUME   D'AVA

ROYAUME   DE LAOS

ROYAUME   DE TUNQUIN

COCHINCHINE

Latitude Septentrionale

Maratha wars

With Mughal power waning, the Maratha Hindu warrior caste took power in western India after 1674. Within a century they controlled most of the subcontinent and had a formidable navy. After Portuguese forces were defeated in 1739, British traders fortified Bombay (Mumbai), expecting attacks. The British East India Company enforced the farming of cotton rather than food crops in Bengal, exacerbating a famine around 1770 in which between 2 and 10 million died. In 1767, Company forces sided with the Maratha against Mysore, and in 1775 they intervened in a succession crisis, depleting British forces available to fight in America. Other powers fought the Maratha; Tipu Sultan allied with the French against them. The second Anglo-Maratha war (1803–5) ended in victory for the future Duke of Wellington and left Maratha lands depleted. A third and final war (1817–18) left the Company *de facto* rulers of India, adapting Mughal bureaucracy. After an 1857 revolt prompted by crass handling of Hindu and Muslim troops, the British government formally took control.

Northwest Indian Wars

Following the Seven Years' War, Britain had tried placating Native American tribes by banning settlements west of the Appalachian mountains. The colonists had disapproved, but the 1783 Treaty of Paris, ending the Revolutionary War, ignored this issue entirely. Several tribes united to negotiate with the new government as the Indian Western Confederacy, claiming the Ohio River as a boundary limit—the USA went to war again in 1785, but made no progress for several years. Keen military strategist Little Turtle defeated American troops in several battles, and Britain quietly supplied the Confederacy with guns.

However, the US army eventually won a decisive victory in the 1794 Battle of Fallen Timbers. The Treaty of Greenville set a boundary and government annuities the following year, but settlers continued pressing west in violation of the agreement. This set the pattern for all subsequent interactions—tribal alliances, warfare, and meaningless treaties that increasingly stripped away native lands, as seen in the Trail of Tears.

The French Revolution

By 1788, with France close to bankrupt, King Louis XVI summoned an Estates-General assembly in a bid to raise new taxes. The "Third Estate" (the commoners) had grown hugely since the last meeting of 1614, but found its powers still restricted. When the Third Estate reformed itself as a National Assembly, Louis was forced to produce a draft constitution, but amid crippling inflation and rumors of martial law most Parisians found this unsatisfactory, and in June 1789, a mob freed mutinous soldiers. Louis mobilized the army but by July 14, when the symbolic Bastille prison was stormed, the tide had turned. The Assembly devised a constitution based on the Declaration of Independence and Enlightenment thinking. New France was to be guided by reason and liberty; even the calendar was decimalized and church estates nationalized to relieve the financial crisis. Louis, however, sought aid from his Austrian Habsburg in-laws. With invasion looming, the rational constitution was suspended and emergency powers introduced —mob rule would be replaced by state Terror.

Chemistry

After the invention of the microscope in the 17th century highlighted the limits of everyday observation, "natural philosophers" sought to refine matter into irreducible elements. Early scholars were as likely to be poets as apothecaries (the Romantic movement exemplifies Enlightenment ambivalence about such divisions). Hydrogen and oxygen were isolated and named by French pioneer Antoine Lavoisier (with hints from Joseph Priestly), nitrogen by Daniel Rutherford; English rioters harassed Priestly, but Lavoisier was beheaded in the Terror.

From the mid-18th century, empirical researchers attempted to examine the material world free of assumptions or received opinion. This led them to be associated, generally correctly, with political radicalism. Yet they were also closely allied to industrial entrepreneurs. In the wake of the Agrarian Revolution the role of chemistry in plant and animal growth was examined. This and the success of metallurgy made links between private scholars and the working lives of millions strong and complex.

The Haber-Bosch process for fixing nitrogen (around 1909) led to a revolution in fertilizers; one-third of the world's food is now linked to it, and in the developed world, half the nitrogen in a human body originates in industrial ammonia plants. Yet Fritz Haber's work also led to chemical weapons and the pesticide used in the Holocaust. Vibrant aniline dyes, the big fashion statement of the 1890s, were developed from aromatic methyls, the same research leading to modern plastics; the complex hydrocarbons of petroleum became the world's main fuel source. Explosives aided road construction but were potent weapons: Alfred Nobel, guilt-stricken inventor of dynamite, instituted awards for Literature, Medicine, and Peace as well as Chemistry and Physics. Factories employed thousands of unskilled laborers, including a higher proportion of women than usual, to make everyday items in life-threatening conditions; disfigurements through exposure to phosphor in match-making, and mercury in hat factories were familiar.

The 20th century accelerated the use of industrial research to develop medicines. Anesthetics and antibiotics saved millions, while increased longevity in the developed world and control over fertility have changed perspectives and practices that seemed fixed since time immemorial.

The Terror

The French Revolution involved considerable violence from the outset, but, with the execution of Louis XVI in 1793, matters accelerated. Britain, Spain, and the Netherlands joined the Austrian offensive; France was fighting for survival. Two factions, the Jacobins and less radical Girondins, sought control; by summer, Jacobin Maximilien de Robespierre's Committee of Public Safety had become France's governing body. Executions of leading figures from both parties followed, and Parisians made increasingly frenetic attempts to prove their loyalty to the Revolution. Thousands were dispatched by the efficient, rational, and democratic guillotine. Discontent grew with the murder of Jean-Paul Marat, and Robespierre himself was executed in July 1794, with the ruling National Committee soon replaced by the Directoire. Meanwhile, war raged (France held its own, capturing the Netherlands); a Corsican, Napoleon Bonaparte, gained renown after saving the Toulon naval base from the British in 1793. As commander-in-chief after 1796, he seized Austria's Italian possessions.

Napoleon in Egypt

After conquering Italy, Napoleon Bonaparte was France's most popular general. Young, charismatic, and ambitious, he embodied Enlightenment ideals. His decision to invade Egypt was as much investigative as military: he sought to depose the Beys and to establish a cultural and scientific *Academie Egyptienne*. Strategic considerations, such as blocking British access to India, justified the sortie, but the Paris Directoire wanted him elsewhere. After he defeated the Mamluks at the Battle of the Pyramids, Britain dispatched Admiral Nelson to the Mediterranean to block supply routes, but Napoleon's forces and "savants" (some 160 scholars and engineers) were already established, working on the monumental *Description D'Egypte*. Nelson's destruction of the French flagship *L'Orient* in the Battle of the Nile changed Bonaparte's plans. Leaving the savants and a military governor to run Egypt, he returned to Paris, where his brother's term as administrator was coming to an end. Within four years, Napoleon declared himself Emperor and launched himself into the conquest of Europe.

Irish rebellion

With the Enlightenment and the French Revolution, Irish discontent over being indentured servants in their own land became politically articulated. Ever since the Ulster Plantations, occasional protests had been suppressed: exemplary punishments meted out by Oliver Cromwell formed a focus for wider complaints about absentee English landlords. The 1690 Battle of the Boyne, in which England's new Dutch monarch William of Orange enforced Protestant rule, led many to side with anyone who stood against England.

The Society of United Irishmen, set up in 1791 by Wolfe Tone, hoped to liberate the nation through an alliance of Catholics and Protestants. This proved untenable, but Tone soon made contact with the French. An attempted invasion in 1796 was defeated by ferocious storms, but the British treated Irish rebels as enemies thereafter, and two 1798 French landing parties were quickly crushed. The 1801 Act of Union brought Ireland under central control as part of Great Britain.

Emperor Napoleon

With Napoleon in Egypt in 1799, another coalition attacked France; Russia temporarily undid French gains in Italy, but withdrew after conflicts with Austria. A returning Napoleon reversed the losses and declared himself First Consul, then Emperor in 1804. After defeating Prussia and Austria (obliterating what remained of the Holy Roman empire), France essentially controlled the continent. There remained Britain and Russia. The 1805 Battle of Trafalgar had wrecked the French and Spanish fleets, allowing the British navy to blockade Europe; in return, Napoleon forbade trade with Britain, but this was economically damaging to both sides. Portugal now allied with Britain, and Napoleon's attempt to put his brother on the Spanish throne triggered the Peninsular War, which continued until 1813. Russia withdrew from the Continental system in 1810, and Napoleon invaded in 1812: his troops took Moscow, but French casualties proved unsustainable. Napoleon raised another army, but now Prussia was in revolt: the Allies invaded France in 1814, and Napoleon was exiled to Elba.

Haitian Revolution

In 1697, France and Spain split possession of the Caribbean island of Hispaniola. Haiti, the French portion, became one of the most profitable colonies in the Americas, exporting coffee, sugar, and cotton, and during the French Revolution its white planters, seeing liberty and fraternity as against their interests, sought independence. In 1791, a slave rebellion broke out: former slave Toussaint L'Ouverture emerged as a capable rebel general, working with French authorities after slavery was abolished. Napoleon, however, planned resuming slavery, and sent troops to Haiti in 1801. War erupted again, but L'Ouverture was captured in 1802. Amid mounting casualties, Napoleon abandoned his plans for an American empire, later negotiating the Louisiana Purchase. Jean-Jacques Dessalines, one of L'Ouverture's officers, triumphed in 1803, massacring the remaining white population. President John Adams supported L'Ouverture, but the US only formally recognized Haiti during the American Civil War. Later, a restored French monarchy demanded reparations, obliterating the young state's economy.

TOUSSAINT LOUVERTURE,

Abolitionists

European states supported slavery until the Enlightenment, as a profitable enterprise, but Judge Mansfield adjudicated in 1772 that nothing in English common law permitted the "odious" practice. Quakers were among the leading Anglo-Saxon voices calling for abolition, while freed slaves and other black activists were also influential. Parliament did not ban trade until 1807, nor slavery itself until 1833. France abolished slavery at home in medieval times, and across its empire after the French Revolution, but Napoleon restored it overseas. Iberia permitted slavery for far longer, and Brazil until 1888. Many countries in Africa (notably those under colonial control, such as the Belgian Congo) had legal slavery into the 20th century.

America enshrined the practice in its Constitution, but abolitionist views became more popular in the northern, industrialized states. Harriet Beecher Stowe's polemic *Uncle Tom's Cabin* became the bestselling novel of the 1800s, and divisions over the practice provoked the American Civil War.

Nigerian-born Olaudah Equiano was enslaved as a child and later shipped
to Virginia, but was eventually able to purchase his freedom in England.
He became a prominent abolitionist campaigner, and his 1792 autobiography,
the *Interesting Narrative*, had a huge influence on its readers.

Louisiana Purchase

Spain had theoretically won the 828,000 square-mile (2.1 million square-kilometer) Louisiana Territory in the Seven Years' War, but only developed the Mississippi river port of New Orleans. France demanded its return in the 1801 Treaty of Aranjuez (though capitulation didn't appease Napoleon for long). However, the French emperor lost his taste for American adventures after Haiti. American farmers needed New Orleans to transport crops, so in 1803 President Thomas Jefferson sent a delegation to Paris to buy the port. Napoleon offered the whole territory for 70 million francs, to fund his war with Britain. Jefferson paid, Spain quibbled fruitlessly—and neither party considered the Native Americans. Jefferson ordered a scientific survey, the Lewis and Clark expedition, which mapped out the country and made contact with dozens of tribes, aided by guide-translator Sacagawea. American delegate James Monroe's eponymous Doctrine two decades later stated that Europe should stay out of the Americas, but the United States wasn't powerful enough to enforce this until later.

Gauchos

Predating US cowboys by a century, the cattle-herders of the South American pampas have a seminomadic culture resembling Eurasia before Genghis Khan. Spanish Conquistadors brought livestock with them—by 1700, there were millions of cattle roaming the grassland and jeopardizing native flora. Gauchos—itinerant expert horsemen—herd the animals for consumption and sale to the European market. Most, but not all, are *mestizos* (of mixed Spanish/native heritage). In Argentina's 1816 War of Liberation, most cavalry on both sides were gauchos; Simón Bolívar recruited many.

As their numbers declined their mystique grew: Argentina's national epic *Martín Fierro* depicts a revolutionary with exemplary independence of mind: fighting Spanish rule and resenting any outsiders are aspects of the solitary lifestyle. While beef production became increasingly industrialized in the 20th century, much of the land is still marginal, suited to migratory grazing and a largely unchanged method of farming.

Waterloo

The allied invasion of France in 1814 forced Napoleon to abdicate. In Vienna, Habsburg foreign minister Metternich negotiated a system of alliances to prevent future uprisings, but restoring Louis XVII was not the immediate panacea France expected. In March 1815, Napoleon escaped exile on the island of Elba, returning with a volunteer army. He immediately invaded Belgium (part of the Habsburg Netherlands) to defend Paris, stop Prussian and British forces rendezvousing, and make a point, but his opponents had defeated him before—Britain's Wellington was canny, Prussia's Blücher (aged 72) fearless.

Napoleon's usual procedure involved precise infantry and artillery strikes; these undertrained peasants and old soldiers were plentiful and willing, but communications broke down. Crucially, he miscalculated the speed of Blücher's advance and strength of his forces. Wellington made best use of theoretically inferior forces until the Prussians broke through. Napoleon was exiled again to St. Helena, dying six years later.

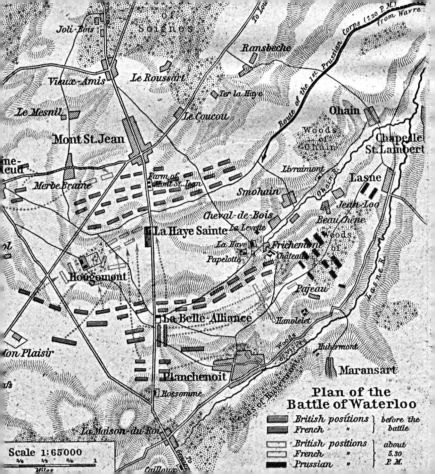

Plan of the
Battle of Waterloo

Scale 1:65000
¼ ½ ¾ 1
Miles

British positions } before the
French   "   } battle

British positions } about
French   "   } 5.30
Prussian   "   } P.M.

Steam

In 1764, while repairing a Newcomen engine, James Watt realized that a separate chamber to condense steam would greatly improve its efficiency. From 1775 he entered partnership with Birmingham businessman Matthew Boulton to produce engines not only for mines, but also for driving wheels hitherto powered by water; factories could now be built anywhere.

By 1814, the use of steam to propel vehicles was being worked on: George Stephenson developed the *Blücher* and later ran the first public steam railroad with the *Rocket* (opposite). Trains crossed Britain within a generation, changing everything from reading habits to local timekeeping. Worldwide, they brought high-capacity freight to and from all corners of Europe, the British, and French empires. America was domesticated by the railroad and the steamboat, the westward surge accelerated by the 1849 Gold Rush. Trains and steam-driven ships mixed races and cultures as never before. Even when electricity became the main power source, the generators ran on steam.

A contemporary engraving of George Stephenson's *Rocket*, which offered the first public steam rail service from 1830.

Simón Bolívar

Arguably the most important figure in Latin American history, Simón Bolívar (1783–1830) inspired the continent's liberation from Spanish dominion. His family had settled in Venezuela in the 16th century, and soon established themselves with large estates and valuable copper mines. Bolívar spent his early years steeped in Enlightenment values, before training as a soldier. Inspired by witnessing the coronation of Emperor Napoleon while in Europe, he returned to Venezuela in 1807 and planned the coup that would see the country declare independence in 1811. The plotters took advantage of Spain's disarray at the time (Napoleon had just invaded), but Spanish forces had rallied and civil war ensued. Bolívar decamped to Haiti before returning in 1816 to begin campaigns that would end in the independence of Gran Colombia (a unified state involving parts of Colombia, Ecuador, Panama, Venezuela, and Peru—the union broke down shortly before his death in 1831). Later he helped liberate the rest of Peru and Bolivia—he would be president of all of these.

Independence in
the Americas:

Before
1800

1800–20

1821

1822–29

1830
onward

Greek independence

Greece had been run by the Ottomans for centuries, but nationalist movements were growing across Europe. An expatriate group, *Filiki Eteria*, stirred sympathy for nationhood among Europeans aware of their debt to classical thought: the London Greek Society alone raised £2.8 million. On March 17, 1821, Greek Orthodox Archbishop Germanos openly rejected Turkish rule: popular unrest soon turned to armed revolt.

The sultan allied with Egypt's Mehmet Ali. Britain and Habsburg Chancelor Metternich resisted aiding the revolt, but individuals (famously French painter Delacroix and Britain's rebel poet Lord Byron, who died there) led volunteers. In 1827, Britain and France agreed with Russia to offer Turkey an armistice, but months later British ships at Navarino were attacked by Egypt's navy: the Egyptian fleet was destroyed. New Tsar Nicholas I's Greek-born foreign minister made a case for solidarity among Orthodox peoples, and Russia declared war on Turkey in 1828. Independence came in 1832: many other groups took note.

Trail of Tears

Andrew Jackson was a beloved war hero in the first of two terms as US president when he signed the 1830 Indian Removal Act, a one-page document that removed all vestiges of Native American sovereignty. Despite European settlement, the spread of disease and conflicts including the Seven Years' War, many Native American tribes remained east of the Mississippi, adapting while preserving their culture (tribes such as the Cherokee established literacy, plantation ownership, and even slaveholding, though the Seminole accepted refugees).

The Act declared that any tribe signing a treaty could be validly moved west, away from valuable land desired by the growing US population. Native Americans were then persuaded to sign treaties (often with invalid puppet leaders, or under pressure). Present-day Oklahoma was set aside as Indian Territory (the federal government would open it to white settlers in 1889), and Native American tribes were forced to march there, on thousand-mile treks that left thousands dead along the way.

DEPARTMENT OF THE INTERIOR
GENERAL LAND OFFICE
HON. THOMAS H. CARTER, COMMISSIONER

INDIAN TERRITORY

Scale of Miles

1891

K   A   N   S   A   S

MISSOURI

T E R Y. OF OKLAHOMA

C H E R O K E E S

CREEK

COUNTRY

A R K A N S A S

C H O C T A W

N A T I O N

T   E   X   A   S

Telegraphy

Sailors had used flags for long-distance communication for centuries, but something more reliable was needed, especially with new railroads to coordinate. In 1837, electronic telegraphs were developed in both Britain and America. Samuel Morse also devised an efficient alphabetical code that became standard. Telegraph systems were soon established across America and Europe, and after several thrilling attempts, a transatlantic cable was permanently established in 1866. Real-time international communications were now possible.

Military applications were obvious: Prussia used the telegraph to immense effect in its Schleswig-Holstein conflicts. By World War I, Britain had established a world-spanning series of cables for its empire. Information relays accelerated share dealings, while journalists rejoiced; many newspapers are still called *The Telegraph*. Even after telephones and radio, the telegraph remained economically important up to the 1980s, when it was finally replaced by telex and then the Internet.

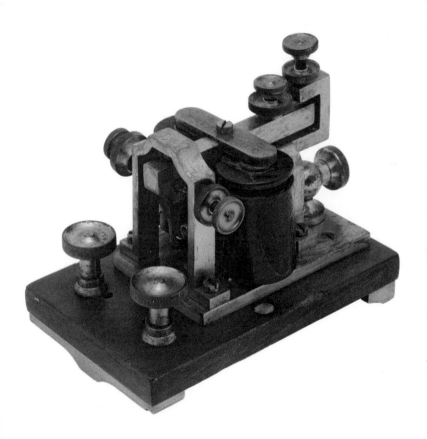

Gold rushes

A peculiarly 19th-century phenomenon links large-scale immigration, the last days of romantic frontier landscapes, and the burgeoning technology that would eliminate them (such as steamships and transcontinental rail links). Following the Mexican–American War, the USA had only just settled its claim to California when James Marshall struck gold at Sutton's Mill in 1848, starting the California Gold Rush: goods were soon being sold at hugely inflated prices, with settlements springing up and flourishing briefly, only to become ghost towns.

Australia's authorities had kept early gold finds quiet for fear of exciting the convict population, but relaxed after seeing the results in California: the country's population nearly tripled in a decade and rose steadily thereafter. Later, a massive influx of non-Boer fortune-seekers to the Transvaal contributed to South Africa's Boer War. Chinese immigration to California was slowed by taxes on foreign miners (many found work in San Francisco, creating the first Chinatown).

Opium Wars

Opium had been introduced to China by Portuguese traders, and Britain wanted Chinese trade goods, particularly highly taxed tea; China would accept only silver in exchange, but US independence ended cheap supplies. With the Manchurian Qing dynasty expanding into Russia and Vietnam, paying an annual $6 million in duty to a rival was not in Britain's interests. Though officially prohibited since 1729, trade in opium (grown by the East India Company) tipped the balance of trade to Britain. In 1839, special commissioner Lin Zexu began to confiscate opium, shutting down the port at Canton. Britain retaliated, overcoming Chinese vessels with its superior navy and guns; 1842's Treaty of Nanking forced China to pay war indemnities, surrender Hong Kong, and open more ports. France joined in with a second conflict from 1857–60 (during the Taiping Rebellion). The 1858 Treaty of Tientsin legalized the opium trade, but China still resisted until Beijing was taken in 1860. Hostilities ended with a treaty surrendering part of Manchuria to Russia—the USA also extracted favorable terms.

The East India Company's iron-clad steamer *Nemesis* (foreground right) had a devastating impact on the opposing Chinese fleet.

Tongan Civil War

Like Thailand, Tonga always maintained indigenous rule (a 1900 British protectorate was honorary). Its main island of Tongatapu has been inhabited for perhaps 5,000 years, and from about AD 950 to 1500 it became a dominant cultural and political power in Polynesia, before declining amid civil war, revolt, and assassinations. The first visiting Europeans were traders from the Dutch East India Company (VOC). In 1799, the tyrannous secular ruler Tuku'aho was assassinated, and conflict began, as local rulers vied to establish themselves.

Finau Feletoa established what amounted to an independent kingdom; his death in 1809 halted hostilities temporarily. Feletoa's son made his son-in-law Taufa'ahau' Tupou' (1797–1893), the grandson of Tuku'aho, heir. Topou's main opponent, the spiritual ruler Laufilitonga, was defeated at the 1826 Battle of Velata. Baptized in 1831 by Wesleyan missionaries, Tupou took the name "George": he went onto eliminate serfdom, establish constitutional monarchy, and form Tonga as a modern state.

King George Tupou I
in his later years.

Universal suffrage

Although the French Revolution and America's Declaration of Independence were couched in Enlightenment rhetoric of inalienable rights, these states were financed by slavery. Following Waterloo, Europe's redrawn boundaries caused dissatisfaction—nationalism was at first allied to progressive causes as an increasingly metropolitan, literate populace demanded a voice. Britain passed a Reform Bill in 1832—elsewhere, the 1848 revolts applied Abolitionist logic to all.

The Tsar Liberator and Habsburgs ended serfdom, and France reabolished colonial slavery, but progress was sporadic—particularly for women. Colorado became the first US state to allow female voting in 1893—with wives no longer considered property, legal objections were spurious. Often, noble ladies could be elected, but not vote: it took World War I to prove that ordinary women could work in hitherto male trades and be entrusted with the vote. Civil Rights acts safeguarding the franchise for US minorities were only established in the 1960s.

1848

It is easier to list parts of Europe that avoided revolution in 1848: Holland, Scandinavia, Britain, and Iberia. Poor harvests, urbanization, and bourgeois dissatisfaction all played their parts, but a significant new element was nationalism. The success of Greek independence inspired Romantic, liberal, and nationalist movements, united against common enemies. New Pope Pius IX raised hopes of reform and news of each revolt spread by telegraph, encouraging others. After rebellion in Vienna, German-speaking principalities set out to form a state —Prussia remained aloof, giving rise to the Schleswig-Holstein Question. Austria remained Habsburg, suppressing Czech independence, but Habsburg and Ottoman plans for Austro-Hungary were thwarted and the region abolished serfdom; Poland gained Habsburg support for its own nationhood; while Italian radical Mazzini forged an improbable alliance of intellectuals and peasants. In France, Louis-Philippe's monarchy ended and Louis-Napoleon, Bonaparte's nephew, was elected president, becoming Emperor Napoleon III in 1852.

Crimean War

As part of their settlement over Greek independence, Russia and the Ottomans had agreed over the latter's Danubian principalities: Russia would base its navy in the Crimea, but abandon European ambitions. But in July 1853, Tsar Nicholas I launched an attack, gambling that France and Britain (even if they bothered to protect Muslims) would never agree a joint mission. He was wrong: Franco-British forces soon arrived at the Dardanelles, and the bolstered Ottomans declared war in October. Austria joined in 1854, forcing Russia's retreat. After thousands of troops died of cholera and a pointless detour to Balaklava, France and Britain pushed onto the naval base at Sevastopol: Russia scuttled its fleet before battle was joined.

This was the first media war: photography and telegraphy came of age, with calamitous misjudgments soon reported in London; Britain's Poet Laureate, Tennyson, wrote "The Charge of the Light Brigade" to attack an infamous "blunder." Modern nursing also began here, with Florence Nightingale and Mary Seacole.

Reportage and photography reaching western
Europe from the front forced commanders
and politicians to consider how the conflict
was presented to the public.

On the Origin of Species

Charles Lyell's studies of geology were already forcing scientists to ponder time in aeons rather than centuries when Charles Darwin (1809–82) studied in Edinburgh. A voyage aboard HMS *Beagle* in the 1830s allowed him to study Galapagos Island finches; he concluded that the many different species must be related, but adapted to local circumstances. He spent two decades refining his theory of "natural selection" —that organisms with beneficial traits are more likely to survive and reproduce, passing on these traits, and leading the species to evolve over time. Darwin finally published in 1858, after Alfred Russel Wallace approached him with a similar idea.

Despite initial controversy over its application to humans, evolution by natural selection quickly became a fundamental axiom in science. Herbert Spencer applied its principles to human society, and Francis Galton invented the term "eugenics" for efforts to improve the human species (later adopted by racists, it was finally discredited after the Holocaust).

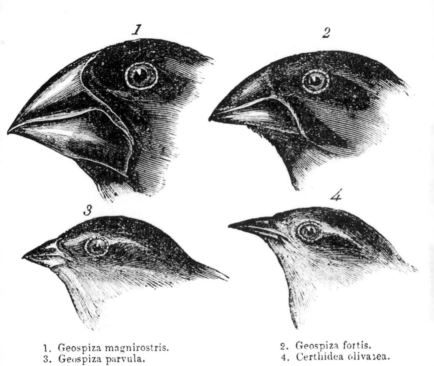

1. Geospiza magnirostris.
2. Geospiza fortis.
3. Geospiza parvula.
4. Certhidea olivasea.

By observing features such as the various shapes of finches' beaks, Darwin concluded that the diversity of species was the result of evolution, not an immutable, divine design.

The *Risorgimento*

After Waterloo, Napoleon's Italian gains were granted to the Habsburgs. However, the city-states and provinces soon became united by a culture of pan-Italian pride (*Risorgimento*, "resurgence") that was opposed by Pope Pius IX. Failed revolts in 1848 motivated Romantic revolutionary movements: Mazzini's "Young Italy" inspired copies in Ireland and Russia. The state of Piedmont formed a model for national government, and in 1859 its prime minister, Count Cavour, wrested Lombardy from Austrian Habsburg rule with the help of Napoleon III. Careerist revolutionary Giuseppi Garibaldi (pictured) brought a force, the Thousand, through Sicily to Naples; Cavour intervened before he could reach Rome, and Garibaldi donated his volunteers and conquests to new head of state King Victor Emmanuel. Italy became a kingdom in March 1861—Cavour died months later. While France supported Italy against the Habsburgs, it had reinforced the papal army against Garibaldi—Rome finally fell in 1870 when the Prussian siege of Paris forced a French withdrawal. By 1871 all of Italy was united—except the Vatican.

Taiping Rebellion

Chinese schoolteacher and failed civil service candidate Hong Xuiquan adopted an idiosyncratic Protestantism and called for commonly held land, rights for women, and an end to footbinding, slavery, opium, and Confucianism. Between 1850 and 1864, his movement established the Taiping Heavenly Kingdom in southeast China, seizing land, conscripting by force, and slaughtering suspected opponents.

Casualty figures are unreliable; the Yangtze and Yellow rivers were disrupted around this time, so plagues and mass starvation, as well as opium casualties and simultaneous rebellions elsewhere, affect the tally. British and French forces supported the Qing rulers: the Hunan army, under Zeng Guofan, was trained by Britain's General Gordon and US mercenary Frederick Townsend Ward. Its scorched-earth policy toward even surrendering cities, combined with Taiping revulsion at the Manchu elite and Confucians, may have left 30 million dead (the contemporary American Civil War killed under a million).

Heavenly Kingdom

American Civil War

The entire United States profited from the "Triangle Trade," but most of the actual slaves were sent to the Southern states for labor-intensive agriculture—especially in cotton production, which accounted for some 60 percent of American exports. Abolitionists, however, gained ground in the industrial North, and when Kansas permitted the decision to be settled by popular vote, the state was flooded with activists, and violence erupted.

A Confederacy of states initially consisting of South Carolina, Mississippi, Florida, Alabama, Georgia, Louisiana, and Texas (Virginia, Arkansas, Tennessee, and North Carolina joined later) seceded after Republican Abraham Lincoln (who had campaigned against the expansion of slavery into free states and US territories, and opposed the growing power of the southern slave states) was elected to presidency. Hostilities commenced when their leader, Jefferson Davis, attacked Fort Sumter, a Union-held fort in South Carolina, on April 12, 1861.

The North was far better equipped for war, possessing most of the country's industrial base, railroads, and the entire navy. The Union's successful blockade stopped exports (and arms smuggling) to the Confederacy. The South, meanwhile, assumed it would gain support from Europe, but in the end no country officially acknowledged the Confederacy—the British textile industry needed cotton, but its solution was to increase production in India.

Much of the military talent, however, went to the Confederacy: Lincoln replaced his generals in rapid succession before finally finding the brilliant Ulysses S. Grant. The South won most conflicts until September 1862; but the Battle of Antietam in Maryland stopped Southern general Robert E. Lee's first incursion on Northern territory.

Soon after, Lincoln drafted the Emancipation Proclamation, proclaiming freedom for slaves in all states a primary aim of the war. Lee's second incursion into the North during 1863 failed at Gettysburg (inspiring Lincoln's famous Address). After Union generals Grant and Sherman began a concerted counterattack, Lee surrendered in April 1865. The war was over, but just days later Lincoln himself was assassinated.

Emperor Maximilian

Napoleon III of France, busy fighting the *Risorgimento*, was aggrieved when Mexico defaulted on its loans in 1862. President Benito Juárez had been struggling with rebels (Mexico had been in chaos since gaining independence in 1821), and with the United States absorbed in its Civil War, this was an ideal time for intervention. Spain and Britain, also burned by the loans, assisted until the grander French plan—to put a Habsburg on the Mexican throne—became clear. Archduke Ferdinand Maximilian had been offered the job in 1859, and a French invasion of Mexico in 1861 prompted fresh requests for restoration of the monarchy. Maximilian I was crowned in 1864.

The reunified US, however, supported Juárez and demanded that European interests stay out of the western hemisphere (deploying 50,000 soldiers to the Rio Grande to reinforce the Monroe Doctrine). France withdrew troops in 1866, and Maximilian's regime fell apart; he was executed by firing squad in 1867. Juárez remained president for the rest of his life.

The fate of the short-lived Emperor Maximilian fascinated French artist Édouard Manet, who produced no fewer than five artworks depicting Maximilian's execution.

The Schleswig–Holstein Question

Having established itself as a major power during the Seven Years' War, Prussia found itself conquered by Napoleon, but reemerged with considerable French territory after Waterloo. Otto Von Bismarck (1815-98), one of history's most capable statesmen (opposite) was appointed chancelor in 1862. He sought to unify the loose German Confederation into a full nation-state, with Prussia dominant over Habsburg Austria. Prussia's army, under Helmuth von Moltke and Albrecht von Roon, was again one of Europe's best, and Bismarck convinced Austria that an alliance against Denmark, which was trying to claim the Schleswig-Holstein duchies, would be in both their interests. The Second Schleswig War ended with the Treaty of Vienna, giving Schleswig to Prussia and Holstein to Austria.

Bismarck now manipulated diplomatic quarrels: an Austro-Prussian war began in 1866, but lasted just two months; Prussia obliterated the Austrians at the Battle of Königgrätz, taking the duchies and pushing Austria out of German politics.

Reconstruction

The American Civil War had exerted huge costs, demanding conscription on both sides and the invention of income tax. The former Confederates were left bankrupt and war-torn, and the newly freed slaves faced huge challenges during the Reconstruction. Various civil rights bills and the Freedmen's Bureau offered help in the first few years. Enthusiastic new voters elected black representatives and senators, but that progressive period ended in 1877: Republican Rutherford Hayes won the presidency with his offer to pull federal troops out of the South, and control over Southern states went with them. Voting restrictions sprang up, white supremacists (the so-called Ku Klux Klan) terrorized black communities, and many African-Americans were forced to become sharecroppers (essentially serfdom). The South remained predominately agricultural for decades. The cultural divide, still unhealed, was accentuated by growing prosperity elsewhere; Mark Twain's 1873 novel *The Gilded Age* encapsulated an era of entrepreneurial monopolies, backroom deals, and corruption.

A satirical cartoon from the Gilded Age criticizes the power wielded over national politics by wealthy industrialists such as John D. Rockefeller.

Xhosa Wars

The source of much future strife in South Africa, a series of nine conflicts escalated from cattle raids and reprisals to all-out war over a century from 1779. The Cape was first colonized by the Dutch VOC, with "Boer Trekkers" (frontier farmers) moving east just as the Xhosa were moving west into the same area. Following assaults by the San, the Boers were merciless when they encountered the Xhosa.

In 1798, the British garrisoned the colony; after Waterloo they were ceded the territory and negotiated with all parties. After a fourth Xhosa attack produced an unexpectedly vicious British response, a 15-year truce prevailed. By the seventh war (1846–7), the Xhosa had guns and both sides used scorched-earth tactics. The eighth followed a teenage girl's disastrous prophecy that Xhosa victory could be assured by sacrificing all their cattle. By the final war (1877–8), the Boers had turned against the British policy of a buffer zone free of white and Xhosa alike, into which the Zulus were now migrating.

Throughout the Xhosa wars, the African tribesmen showed a dangerous reliance on teenage prophetesses such as those shown here, sometimes with disastrous results.

The Tsar Liberator

D espite his repression of Poland, near-genocide in Circassia, and adoption of Siberia as a prison camp, Alexander II is remembered as Russia's most enlightened tsar. His economic and social policies were unprecedentedly liberal and he visited Western nations and most of Russia. After curtailing the Crimean War, his main military action was another war against the Ottomans—this time to liberate Bulgaria.

His policy of ending serfdom, a feudalistic indentured service, established his benign reputation: serfs had been considered property, and ending the system supposedly wrote off the mortgages of landowners: grain exports increased but many bankrupt nobles became bureaucrats. This was to have been the start of a series of reforms analogous to Magna Carta, but Alexander's planned *Duma* (parliament) would not be realized until the next century. Revolutionary cell Narodnaya Volya killed him in a bomb attack in March 1881, instigating draconian reprisals from his son Alexander III and the Kremlin old guard.

Belgian Congo

Both Belgium and Germany believed that African colonies were essential for European powers, and in 1884 they agreed that the Congo, inaccessible and unpromising for previous imperialists, should be a "Free Trade Zone." Belgium's Leopold II set up a company with himself as sole shareholder and began commercial exploitation. In 40 years the population halved. Forced labor to meet strict quotas for palm oil and rubber took men from the land, and anyone not meeting a target was starved, butchered, or saw their children mutilated.

The territory increased with the Treaty of Versailles; German eugenic theories elevated the Tutsi tribe over the Hutu, ultimately leading to the Rwandan genocide of 1994. By 1908, copper had replaced rubber as the focus, and Leopold turned over his holdings to the Belgian government. After World War II, education and welfare systems improved, and in 1960, Belgium finally withdrew; their complicity in the death of elected leader Patrice Lumumba in 1961 warranted an eventual apology.

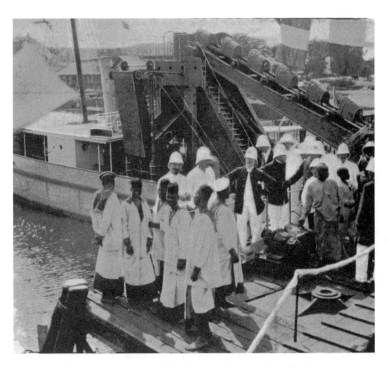

An early photographic album captures a deceptively
serene picture of life in the Belgian Congo.

Ellis Island

The abortive 1848 revolutions and the California Gold Rush saw Europeans depart in their millions to build new lives in America, as the new steam ships allowed cheap, if comfortless, transatlantic passage. A fungal blight had ruined Ireland's potato harvests in the 1840s—a million starved, but twice that moved to England, Australia, and especially America. Pogroms following the assassination of the Tsar Liberator encouraged Russian Jewish emigration. The Homestead Acts, instituted after the Civil War, granted land to those willing to settle and cultivate farms, encouraging western expansion.

The immigrant gateway of Ellis Island was set up in 1892; many newcomers stayed in New York, and it soon rivaled London in population and cultural diversity. The first decade of the 1900s saw the greatest immigration, but the process was not all-inclusive: increasing Chinese immigration to California alarmed local authorities who lobbied for strict quotas on Asians, and general limits were implemented after World War I.

Sino–Japanese Wars

There were two major modern wars between China and Japan, the first from 1894–5, the second from 1937–45 (considered by some to be the true beginning of World War II). After withdrawing from the world during the self-imposed Sakoku Edict, Japan had returned to imperial government after the Meiji restoration and the fall of the Tokugawa shogunate in 1868, and was now establishing itself as an imperial power. Korea provided the first *casus belli*—famine and attempted military coups had made the hitherto independent state vulnerable; when Korea asked its neighbor for troops to help put down the Tonghak Rebellion, Japan claimed a breach of the recently signed Treaty of Tientsin and sent its own expeditionary force, installing a new pro-Japanese government in Seoul.

War followed: China's Ever Victorious Army—a modern force of native soldiers trained under a European officer corps—expected to be easily victorious, but Japan successfully attacked through Korea. After the Imperial Japanese Navy had laid waste to China's Beiyang fleet and gained superiority in the Yellow Sea, troops pushed on into Manchuria, ultimately capturing Taiwan.

In the Treaty of Shimonoseki, China opened its ports, surrendered territory, paid a war indemnity, and acknowledged Korean independence. Japan went onto annexe Korea in 1910, while Manchuria remained officially Chinese, but effectively under Japanese control via local client warlords. Russian aspirations in the area, meanwhile, provoked the Russo-Japanese War.

The second Sino–Japanese War followed. Japan's reconquest of Manchuria began in 1931, but in 1937 a skirmish sparked all-out conflict (albeit undeclared). Japan took Shanghai and the then-capital Nanking, but suffered heavy casualties. The Nanking Massacre is notorious; some 20 million Chinese, civilian and military, died during the war—Japanese losses were perhaps a million. Chinese forces fought guerrilla actions, while Japan attempted to install puppet governments with varying success. Once global hostilities began, the Allies provided aid to China, but largely left this arena alone.

Spanish–American War

Spain's sea power was left diminished after Napoleon's Peninsular Wars. The Philippines rebelled in 1896, and Cuba sporadically from 1868. In 1895 José Martí began a particularly successful guerrilla conflict in Cuba, romanticized by US newspaper chains. As Spain launched a violent suppression, the cruiser USS *Maine* went to Cuba to monitor the situation, only to explode inexplicably on February 15, 1898. US public opinion erupted against Spain; Congress passed the Teller Amendment (promising not to annex Cuba), and declared war on April 25. It was a statement of intent; the USA was now a world power.

The war lasted a mere four months: Spain lacked resources, and more American soldiers died of disease than in battle. The small but sophisticated US navy obliterated the Spanish fleet. America gained all Spain's colonies (Guam, Puerto Rico, and the Philippines) and annexed Hawaii, with Samoa partitioned the next year. The Philippines promptly rebelled again in a war that lasted until 1902—independence only came after World War II.

Boxer Rebellion

Floods, droughts, and famines convinced many in rural China that nature had been unbalanced by outsiders—German and English railroads blocking the *chi*. Discontent brought a return to Taoist traditions and earlier practices. One group, calling themselves "Righteous and Harmonious Fists," rebelled against alien influences, murdering Chinese Christians. At first they had no identifiable leaders or program of action beyond restoration of the old ways and supporting the Qing monarchy against the Manchu court. Millions died, although it was the European casualties who grabbed world attention.

Foreigners and Manchu became a useful focus of discontent among ambitious politicians, notably Dowager Empress Cixi. In June 1900, she ordered death to all foreigners. Japan and Russia sent ships, with Western navies arriving later. After the besieged British Legation complex in Beijing was relieved in July, Cixi denounced the Boxers. European reprisals further destabilized the monarchy, leading to a republic from 1911.

Russo-Japanese War

Following the first Sino-Japanese War, Russia forced Japan to let China keep Port Arthur, then seized it themselves (their only warm-water Pacific port). They profited from the Boxer Rebellion, claiming Manchuria, and started investigating Korea, which Japan regarded as its territory. The Trans-Siberian Railroad would soon give Russia easier troop transport, so Japan preemptively attacked Port Arthur on February 8, 1904. The siege lasted seven months, but Japan sank Russia's eastern fleet and held its own in land actions, including the 1905 Battle of Mukden. When the Baltic fleet finally arrived, it was promptly sunk in the Battle of Tsushima. Facing internal rebellion, Russia signed a peace treaty, withdrew from Manchuria, surrendered Port Arthur, and recognized Japan's claim to Korea.

World reaction was astonishment; 19th-century geopolitics was governed by fear of Russia, but now a non-Western power had proven a serious competitor. The delighted Japanese would eventually overestimate their military capacity in World War II.

A contemporary Japanese illustration shows Russian battleships

Polar exploration

The Northwest Passage (first sailed by Norwegian Roald Amundsen in 1906) inspired navigation of the Arctic seas; Antarctica's discovery in 1820 prompted curiosity. Science and imperialist pride encouraged expeditions to both poles (most European powers sent at least one, plus Japan and America). Rival Americans Frederick Cook and Robert Peary claimed the North Pole in 1908–9—Peary's claim was accepted then, but remains controversial. The first nuclear-powered submarine, USS *Nautilus*, sailed beneath the polar ice cap in 1957–8.

In Antarctica, Britain's Captain Scott made several expeditions, often accompanied by his colleague and rival Ernest Shackleton. During the 1912 *Terra Nova* expedition, Scott led a party to the Pole, only to find Norway's flag already there —Amundsen had reached the Pole weeks before. Scott's team died during their return, but were lauded as heroes. Shackleton, meanwhile, gained renown for saving his entire crew during the doomed *Endurance* expedition.

Mass production

The spread of factories led to hugely accelerated rates of production. Theories of "scientific" manufacture flourished in the 1890s; Frederick Winslow Taylor's time studies and Frank and Lillian Gilbreth's filmed motion analysis spurred development. Henry Ford developed the production-line system, reducing construction time for his Model T automobile from 14 hours to 93 minutes by treating employees as components in a car-making machine, each performing a single repetitive task. The system aided wartime security, preventing workers knowing enough to let slip information, but was alienating. The Soviets sought to make work ennobling and utopian, but to little avail.

The US economy came to rely on unskilled labor making goods for a bottomless market: hence advertising, fashion, built-in redundancy, and Marshall Aid to bolster economies after World War II. Germany, then Japan, adapted the process and beat the USA on price, then quality. In turn, China and Brazil won global markets at the cost of their environments and workers' rights.

Mass media

Magic lanterns for projecting still pictures date to the early 1800s, but the illusion of movement required flexible transparencies for rapidly refreshing images. Celluloid, used in shirt collars, proved ideal: in Lyons, France, Auguste and Louis Lumière developed a portable camera/projector utilizing sewing-machine components and showed the results to paying audiences. From 1895, they sent operators around the world, showing movies they had already taken and adding each new place to the library. Early movies set motion in a static frame; moving the camera added dynamism. Soon, editing techniques made longer, more "authored" works possible.

The 19th century also saw scientists investigate links between electricity and magnetism: Heinrich Hertz induced sparks across a few yards, then Guglielmo Marconi reproduced the effect across longer distances using a long cable antenna. Engineers soon experimented with sound broadcasts carried on modulated waves, and broadcast music began on Christmas

Eve, 1906. The 1910 arrest of the murderer Dr. Crippen using ship-to-shore Morse was noteworthy, but the age of radio really began after Marconi's device saved 700 passengers from the *Titanic* in 1912. Lee de Forest's invention of the triode added amplification. Manufacturers sold domestic kits and also established companies to send entertainment and news.

Philo Farnsworth and Vladimir Zworykin developed the first systems for broadcasting images, but Scotland's John Logie Baird stimulated public interest with his semimechanical process. In 1936, the British Broadcasting Corporation (BBC) evaluated the Baird system and EMI's all-electronic method (suspiciously like Farnsworth's), with the latter proving more resilient. Nazi Germany had a state-run cable network, relaying entertainment and the 1936 Olympics to movie theaters rather than allowing domestic use. America, experimented with cable at the 1939 World's Fair, and had commercial television by 1941 and color transmissions from the 1950s.

Seeing live images of events, eventually via satellites, made appearances ever more important—entertainment became more lucrative than heavy industry, and English became the most widely spoken language.

Panama Canal

The economic benefits of a canal connecting the Pacific and Atlantic oceans at the narrow isthmus in Central America were obvious. An American, William Walker, had even attempted to conquer Nicaragua and briefly declared himself president, interrupting Cornelius Vanderbilt's plans to build a canal there. Colombia owned the territory of another promising region for a canal, present-day Panama, and allowed France to pursue a construction project there—but without adequate technology or men, huge sums and lives were lost.

Under President Theodore Roosevelt (celebrated for his service in the Spanish–American War), the USA thought it could do better. In 1903, it sponsored Panama's independence from Colombia (much to the latter's anger), then took over the region as a protectorate. The canal was finished by 1914, and was one of the largest engineering projects in the world. It was also the first of that century's many US government interventions into Latin American sovereignty (see Allende).

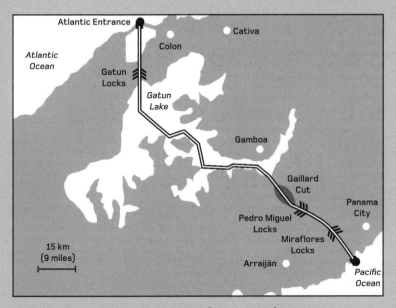

The Panama Canal runs for 48 miles (77 kilometers) across the Isthmus of Panama, connecting the Pacific and Atlantic oceans and dramatically shortening trade routes.

World War I

The Balkan states had driven the Ottomans out of Europe, with Serbia gaining the best spoils; nearby Habsburg Austria-Hungary declared war after a Serbian nationalist assassinated Archduke Franz Ferdinand on June 28, 1914. Russia, the other dominant power in the region, mobilized its forces in case of Austro-Hungarian opportunism, while the Ottomans joined the Central Powers (Germany and Austria-Hungary). Germany, hoping to carve an empire, had been planning for a two-front war since the days of Bismarck, and quickly invaded Belgium for a march into France (which had itself allied with Russia and Britain in the Triple Entente). Everyone expected a brief war, yet by November 1918's Armistice about 16 million had died.

This was the first industrial war: modern military technology came into its own, with tanks, submarines, barbed wire, poison gas, machine guns, and airplanes. German tactics initially succeeded, but the Battle of the Marne stopped their advance just outside Paris; the Western Front stagnated into four years of trench warfare. The Central Powers prospered in the east, however, where incompetent Russian leadership allowed many German victories, and ultimately drove Russia out of the war after the October Revolution.

The dominant British navy blockaded the continent: after the 1916 Battle of Jutland weakened their surface fleet, German naval efforts were confined to submarines, which cut off British shipping (requiring British rationing in 1917). The Allies (notably Britain and its colonies) attempted to open a new front at Gallipoli, near Crimea, in order to block the Ottomans. A 1916 German offensive at Verdun (France) failed, killing thousands in days, and the Germans retreated to defensive positions on the Hindenburg Line in 1917.

Woodrow Wilson had been reelected as US president after promising to keep America out, but indiscriminate submarine attacks and the Zimmerman Note (an invitation for Mexico to join the Central Powers) brought America into the war in 1917. The war wound down after a final German offensive in spring 1918. The Treaty of Versailles is sometimes seen as marking a quarter-century pause, with World War II as a continuation.

Gallipoli

After the Ottomans joined Germany in World War I, British and French possessions such as Mesopotamia and the Suez Canal were clearly vulnerable. For the Triple Entente, opening the Dardenelles strait linking the Mediterranean and Black seas would help protect Russian ships at Odessa and offer a chance to take Constantinople, ideally with a naval campaign. Bad weather and mines prevented this, however. By April 1915, an invasion force had gathered in Egypt—mostly French and British (with one Irish division), but reinforced by the Australia and New Zealand Corps (Anzacs) and India. Early assaults saw Ottoman setbacks, but the campaign eventually lapsed into stalemate. Anglo-French forces withdrew to attack Greece after Bulgaria allied to the Central Powers. While Ottoman and British casualties were immense, the Anzacs suffered disproportionately high losses; Australian politics is still affected. The defeat caused the British government to fall and stimulated fresh fighting in other Ottoman territories. Russia, however, left the war after the October Revolution.

Easter Rising

In the late 19th century, British political parties considered limited Home Rule for Ireland, making independence a real prospect. Unhappy northern Protestants raised militias and threatened armed revolt, but despite this, limited devolution was granted in 1914—only to be suspended with World War I.

The Protestant militias provoked similar militarization among Irish nationalists, armed by Germany. An insurrection began on Easter Monday 1916 with the seizure of key locations in Dublin and shooting of unarmed police. Martial law was declared amid looting, with one British officer summarily executing noncombatants. By the following Saturday, when the rebels surrendered, shelling and gunfire had killed over 500 and wounded thousands. Fifteen were executed for treason and thousands interned. Two years later, the Irish Republican Army (IRA) was formed: war began in 1919, and an exhausted Britain proposed a treaty establishing the Irish Free State, not fully independent. The new state was engulfed in civil war until 1923.

Crowds outside the Dublin Bread Company, badly damaged during the Rising.

October Revolution

A German-born tsarina, mllions of casualties in an unpopular war, famine, and widespread strikes fomented revolt in Russia—not least within the army. The last Romanov tsar, Nicholas II, was forced to abdicate in February 1917, with a provisional government set up that continued fighting against Germany. However, Vladimir Lenin's Bolshevik communists now rose to prominence in the ongoing political struggles, as further revolts and an attempted military coup weakened central control. In October (per the old Russian calendar —November for everyone else) Bolshevik forces seized the center of government, the Winter Palace, with little bloodshed. The Soviet Congress came to power, and the Romanovs were executed the following year. In March 1918, the Treaty of Brest-Litovsk allowed Russia to withdraw from World War I at a price. Civil war began in earnest after Western powers offered the anticommunist "White Russian" troops and aid against the Red Russian forces. Resistance continued until 1922, when the Soviet Union (USSR) officially came into being.

Lenin (center) and other Soviet leaders gathered in Moscow on the second anniversary of the October Revolution.

"Spanish flu" pandemic

The worst pandemic since the Black Death killed at least 50 million people (more than the casualties in World War I, or the death toll of AIDS sufferers) and infected millions more. Its origin remains uncertain (it was dubbed "Spanish flu" because the press in neutral Spain, with no war reporting to do, were first to cover it extensively), but it spread rapidly in the unhygienic trenches of World War I.

The death toll was partly down to sheer virulence; unlike normal influenza, this particular mutation seems to have affected young, healthy people, such as soldiers, more than the old and young. Improved global communications (especially troop movements) soon spread it worldwide; infection was rampant in British India, for instance. Several different waves manifested, one as late as 1920, after which the strain died out. Americans suspected German biological warfare; the Central Powers were much weakened by inflated casualties. Yet the pandemic's sheer rapidity also allowed it to be swiftly forgotten.

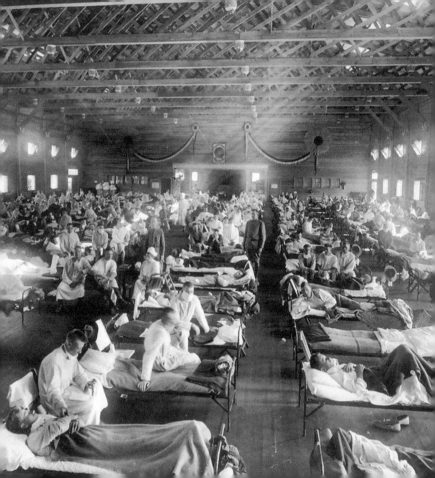

Treaty of Versailles

Paris, 1919: following World War I, an international legation redrew the map of Europe, donating former German territory to other countries (including the Czech Sudetenland, parts adjoining Poland, and overseas colonies). A clause placed blame for the war on Germany and its allies: Austria, the original combatant, was a shadow of its former self. Terms included the payment of severe war indemnities, limitations on the military, and a ban on rearmament. The treaty infuriated Germany and devastated its economy; Hitler later used it as a rallying cry.

The mood was that the four-year carnage must have been for *something*: the "War to End All Wars" should produce a global commitment to peacekeeping. A new organization, the League of Nations, first met in 1920, but US President Woodrow Wilson failed to convince his own nation to join his brainchild, hobbling it from the outset. In the 30s, the Sino-Japanese War, Abyssinia and the Spanish Civil War demonstrated its incapacity. Post-1945 successor the United Nations would be more credible.

Denmark

North
Schleswig

West Prussia

Finland

Estonia

Latvia

Lithuania

Germany

Poland

Pozen

Upper Silesia

Alsace-
Lorraine

France

Czechoslovakia

Austria

Hungary

Romania

Switzerland

Italy

Romania

New or successor states created
by the Treaty of Versailles

Mustafa Kemal Atatürk

The Ottoman empire suffered a long decline: the Balkans rebelled in 1875, Russia invaded again in 1877, and several states were taken by Austria-Hungary or made independent at the Congress of Berlin. Egypt had been largely autonomous for a century before Britain occupied it in 1882. In 1908, the Young Turk Revolution overthrew the sultan. One revolutionary, Kemal Atatürk (1881–1938), became known as a great general in World War I and the subsequent Turkish War of Independence, after the Allies partitioned the empire and occupied Constantinople.

Ottoman refugees fled to Anatolia, which became the core of a new Turkish republic in 1923, with Atatürk as its president. He modernized along nationalist lines, renaming Constantinople Istanbul, outlawing Sharia courts and the Fez, but not the Hijab. The sultanate was abolished, and a secular government created with female suffrage, a Latinized alphabet, and public education. Neutrality during World War II protected the country, and secular, democratic government proved resilient.

Stalin

After the October Revolution, Lenin presided over the Union of Soviet Socialist Republics (USSR) until his death in 1924. He recommended that communist party general secretary Joseph Stalin (1879–1953), be removed, but Stalin avoided this, and after political struggles, exiled his rival Leon Trotsky in 1929 (he was murdered in 1940). He annihilated opposition, exiling dissidents to Siberian labor camps, repeatedly purging the army (weakening its leadership), and staging show trials on an industrial scale. Efforts to industrialize included mass relocations to remote new cities. Attempts to modernize agriculture were catastrophic; collectivization of farms in the 1930s and pursuit of bogus genetic theories starved millions.

The West's preference for Germany as a bulwark against the USSR was a significant factor in the Annexation; conversely, Stalin's pact with Hitler left him unprepared for German attack. Once allied to Roosevelt and Churchill, he preserved the USSR and considerably expanded its postwar sphere of influence.

Great Depression

Wall Street's 1929 stock market crash, analogous to the South Sea Bubble, came as a shock after a decade of American prosperity based on mass production. President Herbert Hoover's ambitious economic policies, and *laissez-faire* removal of banking controls, caused the collapse, and as farms were hit by bank closures, the Dust Bowl was another blow. A quarter of the workforce became unemployed, many ending up in shanty towns called "Hoovervilles." In 1933, new President Franklin Roosevelt began the New Deal—employment schemes and social reforms. This created the infrastructure for modern governmental programs, such as Social Security. European economies, still fragile after World War I, were catastrophically damaged. Inflation in Germany meant sacks of paper notes bought one loaf of bread. Britain devalued its currency, but union action and sympathy from more affluent citizens slowly rebuilt the economy; radios, cars, and the movie theater stimulated growth. Across Europe, demagogues used the crisis to promote a new authoritarian philosophy called "fascism."

Dust Bowl

Technological advances (most importantly cheap steel for railroads and sturdy ploughs) had made the western USA increasingly attractive to settlers in the wake of the American Civil War. Cattle ranching was initially popular, until barbed wire and overgrazing made farmers competitive with cowboys. Wet weather in the 19th century encouraged farmers to use all the land they could (ploughing over moisture-retaining prairie and removing trees). When drought began in 1930, the dry fields quickly eroded. Over the next few years dust storms tore away fertile topsoil across Texas and Oklahoma. "Black Sunday," April 14, 1935, when storms blew dirt across the whole continent, provoked a newspaper editor to coin the term "Dust Bowl."

Farming was thus unable to soften the blow of the Great Depression. Millions lost their land, fleeing to California or Florida. Congress passed an act requiring conservation, but the US economy only truly recovered in the 1940s, when the rains returned and the country entered into World War II.

Spanish Civil War

The last time a country came close to turning communist before the Cold War (see Mao) became something of a proxy war. Spain abolished its monarchy after democratic elections in 1931, but an attempted military coup in 1936 set the stage for a brutal conflict with hundreds of thousands of casualties. Germany supported the fascist, pro-Catholic Nationalist side and Russia the left-leaning Republic—Western democracies officially stayed out, but individuals came to support both sides, notably writers (Orwell, Hemingway, Auden, and many others) who witnessed the Republic's "International Brigade" turning on itself. Germany sent Stuka dive bombers, terrifying Western leaders and inspiring Picasso's depiction of the destruction of Guernica. The Nationalists had won by 1939.

Nationalist leader Francisco Franco became dictator for life. He kept Spain largely neutral during World War II and a period of reconstruction followed. On his death in 1975, Juan Carlos become king, with democracy reestablished soon after.

JUNTA DELEGADA DE DEFENSA
DE MADRID
DELEGACIÓN DE PROPAGANDA Y PRENSA

Abyssinia

Unified Italy looked on as other European states carved up Africa. It had taken Libya and some small eastern lands, but was humiliatingly defeated in an 1896 attempt to take Ethiopia, the former center of the Abyssinian empire, between Italian Eritrea and Somalia. In 1935, new leader Benito Mussolini, modeling himself on Julius Caesar and founding a movement he termed "fascism," declared his intention to finish the job. Both countries were signatories of the League of Nations and of the Kellogg pact (outlawing war between members), and Ethiopia's Emperor Haile Selassie counted on Britain and France to block Italy, but sanctions proved useless, since America had not joined the League. Barefoot infantry resisted Mussolini's tank battalions; Selassie threw his resources behind them, trusting Britain to honor its treaty obligations. But when Italy sent in bombers, the League was revealed as worthless. The Sino-Japanese War's devastation of Manchuria compounded this, encouraging Hitler to abandon the Treaty of Versailles. Ethiopia was liberated during World War II.

Annexation of Sudetenland

Following the Treaty of Versailles, the German government of the Kaiser was replaced by the Weimar Republic, but by 1930 hyperinflation was devastating the economy; many fringe parties offered solutions. Following Mussolini's lead, Adolf Hitler (1889–1945) established a fascist power base by adopting left-wing rhetoric. His Nazi Party gained power and he became chancelor in 1933. Nazis offered many scapegoats for Germany's weakness, especially communists and Jews: when a fire devastated the Reichstag parliament building, Hitler blamed communists and won dictatorial powers. Seeking to regain lost German territory, in 1935 Hitler seized the French-controlled Saar Basin, occupying the Rhineland in 1936. His homeland of Austria joined Germany in 1938, and next he went after German-speaking Sudetenland, now part of independent Czechoslovakia. The League of Nations proved powerless, and Britain, France, Germany, and Italy signed the appeasing "Munich Agreement," surrendering the Sudetenland. Germany still invaded the rest of Czechoslovakia in 1939.

World War II

The generation of European leaders who had experienced World War I would try anything to prevent a repetition, and thus the ambitious Axis powers (Italy, Japan, and Germany) gained concessions. Hitler had at least an arguable claim to the Sudetenland but Britain's Neville Chamberlain calculated that no sane leader would risk all-out war over the relatively slight prize of Poland, which had allied to Britain and France.

By the time Germany did indeed invade Poland on September 1, 1939, Chamberlain had at least bought time to rearm. German *blitzkrieg* ("lightning war") tactics proved effective; the USSR (briefly allied to Germany) moved in from the east, and Poland was split in two. In April 1940, Germany took Denmark and invaded Norway (necessary for the supply line to Swedish metal ore). The effort destroyed much of their surface fleet, and naval efforts thereafter involved harassing Allied convoys with U-boats, forcing rationing that continued in Britain until 1954. France threw its resources into fortifications, but German forces bypassed the "Maginot Line" by invading through Belgium, again obliterating opposition. The remaining Allied forces evacuated from Dunkirk, and France surrendered in June 1940, with the pliant "Vichy" government taking over. A resistance movement (led by General de Gaulle) continued.

Germany now sought air superiority over the English Channel in order to invade Britain; it began the Battle of Britain with more planes, but the Royal Air Force held them off (and Hitler emphasized bombing London over English airfields). Mussolini, meanwhile, incautiously expanded Italy's African ambitions and invaded Greece—resulting complications drained resources from Germany as it attacked the Soviet Union in 1941. The Allies (joined by America after Pearl Harbor) pushed the Italians back in Africa, and German General Rommel was soundly beaten at El Alamein in 1942. After invading Italy in 1943, the Allies took Rome on June 4, 1944 (Mussolini was eventually executed by partisans). Two days later came D-Day; Allied forces stormed Normandy and spent the rest of the year retaking France. December's "Battle of the Bulge" was the last major German offensive; thereafter they retreated on all fronts. As Soviet troops entered Berlin, Hitler shot himself on April 30, 1945, and Germany surrendered nine days later. Over 60 million died in all.

Stalingrad and Leningrad

The *blitzkrieg* tactic had brought the Nazis quick victory in France and Poland—despite German-Soviet nonaggression treaties, Hitler planned the same for the USSR. Operation Barbarossa began on June 22, 1941, with army groups ordered to take Moscow and Leningrad (formerly St. Petersburg). The Russian army had been weakened by Stalin's various military purges and the Winter War conflict with Germany's ally Finland. German troops encircled Leningrad by September but were redeployed to help assault Moscow. The invaders were caught by winter (like Napoleon), and failure to take Moscow ended Hitler's hopes for a rapid victory. Leningrad was besieged until 1944, while a 1942 offensive, taking Stalingrad (Volgograd) and rich southern oilfields, also ultimately failed after some of the war's bloodiest fighting. Germany was now overstretched, while USSR industrial capacity and military conscription increased. After German retreat at Kursk, the next two years saw Soviet advances. In 1945 the Soviets took East Germany and Berlin (importantly for the Cold War), ending the European conflict.

Pearl Harbor

With its decision not to join the League of Nations after the Treaty of Versailles, America had set itself on a path of geopolitical isolationism after World War I. However, as the rest of the world became swept up in World War II, President Franklin Roosevelt had persuaded Congress to provide Britain with "Lend-Lease" aid, located a fleet in Hawaii to protect US interests and, in June 1941, signed executive orders freezing Axis war assets.

Even after Lend-Lease assistance was extended to the USSR in November 1941, Germany would have gained nothing from engaging America. Its fellow Axis power Japan, however, would: 90 percent of its oil, along with iron imports necessary for its war effort, had previously come from the US—with Roosevelt's actions cutting off these supplies, the militaristic forces in the government felt that the best option was to invade Indonesia, rich in oil, and try to knock out the American fleet quickly.

The air strike of December 7, 1941 on the US military base in Pearl Harbor, Hawaii, came as a complete surprise: even Japan's Washington embassy only decoded the declaration of war after the attack had begun (US codebreakers were quicker, and only just missed giving warning). Two thousand soldiers died, and several battleships were sunk (though no aircraft carriers—a factor that would prove important in the enormous Pacific theater of war). An outraged American public was suddenly willing to fight. Germany and Italy's declarations of war on December 11 drew America into the European theater as well—European aid greatly increased thereafter, and the USA properly joined the Allied conflicts in North Africa in 1942.

Within the Pacific, Japan had considerable early success, keeping US forces at stalemate in the May 1942 Battle of the Coral Sea, but it lost the initiative and critical carriers in the Battle of Midway. Japan also wrested strategically-vital Singapore and Burma from Britain. The Japanese fought on defensively (losing most of their fleet in the Philippines in 1944) until, rather than risk the casualties associated with a direct Allied invasion, America dropped nuclear bombs on Hiroshima and Nagasaki in 1945. Japan surrendered on August 15, 1945, finally bringing World War II to an end.

Gandhi and Churchill

Winston Churchill reported on the Boer War and came to believe in the British empire as a modern Pax Romana. Mohandas K. Gandhi, in contrast, trained as a lawyer in India and worked in South Africa, seeing the empire at its worst. After corresponding with Leo Tolstoy, he developed an idea of passive resistance to achieve political change, uniting Tolstoy's "Civil Disobedience" with Hindu beliefs, and adopted the loincloth that would be his trademark. Other Indian independence activists, notably Nehru and Bose, distrusted his demagoguery.

In early 1942, after Singapore's surrender to Japan, Churchill sent Stafford Cripps to negotiate with Indian politicians. Cripps offered dominion status after the war, analogous to Canada and interwar Ireland. Bose mustered Indian POWs in Singapore to fight against Britain. When Japan invaded Burma, supplies that might have fed those starving around Calcutta were diverted on Churchill's orders. At least 3 million died, with many directly attributable to Churchill's intransigence.

Holocaust

From 1938, a variety of people deemed "undesirables" under Nazi ideology were sent into concentration camps: Roma, gay men, anyone with a disability. Bolsheviks were interned and killed but the emphasis, numerically and culturally, was on Jews. Germany, like many other Western countries, had considerable anti-Semitic sentiment; fascism nurtured it, developing the pseudoscience of eugenics into an ideology of Aryan power and purity that demanded the destruction of all else.

After the 1941 invasion of the Soviet Union, the Nazis decided more drastic steps were required: a "Final Solution." Victims were transported to death camps maintained by Himmler's SS, and gassed *en masse* using the odorless pesticide Zyklon B. More than 9 million Jews lived in Europe before World War II (most in Eastern Europe and Germany). By 1945, two-thirds had died; the final toll is uncertain. The full horror was not known in the West until the end of the war, when journalists accompanied troops liberating Auschwitz and Buchenwald.

Hiroshima and Nagasaki

Atomic fission was widely understood to be capable of releasing vast amounts of energy, but in 1933, Leó Szilárd produced a working model of the nuclear chain reactions required. Szilárd was a pacifist, but fearing that the Nazis might develop such a weapon first, he and Albert Einstein convinced President Roosevelt to fund the Manhattan Project —an international effort led by Robert Oppenheimer. The atomic age began with the Trinity Test in New Mexico on July 16, 1945, and Roosevelt died with Einstein's proposal of a test on an uninhabited island, inviting the Axis powers' surrender, on his desk. His successor, Harry Truman, decided a direct use of the new weapon would end the Pacific war more quickly (and demonstrate American power to the Soviets). Bombs were dropped on the Japanese cities of Hiroshima and Nagasaki on August 6 and 9: at least 200,000 died as a result, and Japan surrendered on September 2. Despite secrecy, the USSR had its own nuclear bomb by 1949. Einstein, Oppenheimer, and others spent the rest of their lives campaigning against proliferation.

Partition

Since World War I, the question had been not *whether* India should be independent but *how*. With US President Truman demanding immediate repayment of wartime loans and Churchill voted out of office, Britain could no longer afford its empire. Nehru and Gandhi demanded a unified state, but the minority Muslim population, fearing genocide in a Hindu nation, demanded partition. The 1905 Curzon Plan had floated a notional Muslim "Pakistan' "but Sikhs were concentrated in Punjab, a majority-Muslim northern state, particularly around Lahore and Amritsar. King George VI's popular cousin, Lord Mountbatten, was imposed as the last Viceroy of India as British troops began to withdraw. Independence was set for August 15, 1947, and a day earlier for the various Pakistani territories including modern Bangladesh. Borders were based on populations and locations of rivers and railroads—had they been announced earlier, massacres might have been prevented. Mobs "cleansed" cosmopolitan cities, including Lahore, and a million out of 15 million refugees created by Partition died.

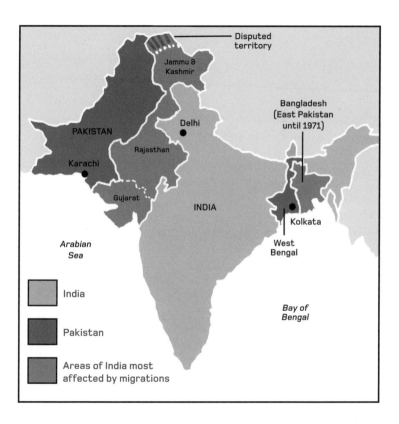

Disputed territory

Jammu & Kashmir

PAKISTAN

Delhi

Rajasthan

Karachi

Gujarat

INDIA

Bangladesh
(East Pakistan
until 1971)

Kolkata

West
Bengal

*Arabian
Sea*

*Bay of
Bengal*

India

Pakistan

Areas of India most
affected by migrations

Israel and Palestine

Support for a Jewish homeland of Israel had grown through the 19th century in European countries and among the Jewish diaspora. After World War I and the dissolution of the Ottoman empire, Britain took control of Palestine, to the anger of an Arab population who had hoped for independence. Territory beyond the Jordan River was eventually set aside for the Arabs (still effectively under British control). By the 1930s, Britain was attempting to maintain control by restricting Jewish immigration as tens of thousands fled Europe. The Arabs revolted anyway in 1936, and Britain had barely put down the rebellion by the time World War II began. The Transjordan gained independence as Jordan in 1946, while revulsion at the Holocaust led the UN to back the establishment of Israel in 1947. Hundreds of thousands of Arabs expelled from the area became refugees. When the British pulled out in 1948, the surrounding nations, unified in the Arab League, attacked. Despite UN intervention, war continued until 1949, but Israel prevailed and was soon flooded with Jewish settlers from around the world.

Mao

Weakened by the Boxer Rebellion, China's Qing dynasty collapsed in 1911. Long-time revolutionary Sun Yat-sen became president of a republic, until army officer Yuan Shikai forced him into exile. Chaos ensued, but after Shikai died, Sun returned to advocate unification. His supporters, the Kuomintang, succeeded in the 1926–8 Northern Expedition military campaign, and after his death Chiang Kai-shek became leader. Mindful of his financial support from capitalists in Shanghai, he purged the communists, killing thousands. Civil war erupted again, and former student revolutionary Mao Zedong (1893–1976) became a key opposition military leader. The Sino-Japanese War forced some cooperation, but conflict resumed after Japan surrendered. Communists, promising land to the populace, ultimately conquered the country: Maoism differed from Marxist-Leninism by emphasizing agriculture over industry. Mao declared the People's Republic of China in 1949, cementing his power with mass executions and labor camps as the remaining Kuomintang fled to Taiwan.

毛泽东
MAO ZE DONG
1893·12·26 —— 1976·9·9

Berlin Airlift

Immediately after World War II, Germany was divided into blocs, with the Soviets taking the east and extracting harsh reparations. Berlin lay within this zone, but was itself divided among the wartime allies. When France, America, and Britain united their territories to create the Federal Republic (West Germany) in June 1948, Stalin cut off all land access to West Berlin. The city was supplied via an airlift that landed several thousand tons of supplies by air every day for 11 months, before Stalin relented. Identifying their one-time ally as a new threat, the other powers set up the North Atlantic Treaty Organization (NATO)—the beginnings of the "Cold War."

A reinvigorated West Germany became a focus for trade deals, central to the European economy. Soviet premier Khrushchev sanctioned construction of a huge wall to isolate West Berlin in 1962. The city became a magnet for artists and entrepreneurs, and a hotbed of espionage. Demolition of the wall by protesters signaled the impending collapse of the Soviet Union in 1989.

Korea

After World War II ended, the USA and USSR took control of war-torn areas they judged incapable of self-rule, occasionally partitioning them (hence the Berlin Airlift). Korea, however, had been an independent nation for centuries until Japan annexed it soon after the first Sino-Japanese War. US diplomat Dean Rusk arbitrarily suggested Korea be split along the 38th parallel, with the USSR monitoring the northern half and the USA handling the south. Both countries installed governments friendly to their political beliefs, which soon came into conflict, and communist North Korea invaded South Korea in 1950. The USA and Europe supported the South with troops, while Mao's new People's Republic of China sent men to the North. In 1953, the "police action" ended in an exhausted armistice, with 3 million dead (mostly Koreans) and a demilitarized zone, roughly following the same parallel where the conflict had started, which remains today. Aside from demonstrating the UN's inability to impose peace, this was the first of many Cold War proxy conflicts.

Indochina

Cambodia's King Huang enlisted Napoleon III's help to thwart Vietnamese and Thai imperialism. Thailand later played imperialists off against each other, and Britain fought to retain Burma, but from the 1860s, Vietnam, Laos, and Cambodia were French protectorates. In 1946, France tried to resume its "protection," only for communist revolutionary Ho Chi Minh to declare a Democratic Republic of Vietnam in the north. The anticommunist south, meanwhile, asked for French aid.

The First Indochina War lasted from 1946 to 1954; France withdrew after the Battle of Dien Bien Phu. America, occupied in Korea, provided financial aid and military advisors. The Geneva Conference suggested a temporary division of north and south, with free elections later. However, Ngo Dinh Diem stole the southern election, becoming dictator until his assassination in 1963. Fighting resumed with the South enlisting American aid. The Vietminh, Southern insurgents, fought successful guerrilla actions and were eventually aided by the North.

Mau Mau Rebellion

Under the British Empire, Kenya had become home to many European settlers. A secret society, the Mau Mau, formed in 1947 among the Kikuyu trube, aimed to oust them. At first, burglary and arson were treated as simple crimes, but after Chief Waruhiu was speared to death for condemning them in 1952, Governor-General Sir Evelyn Baring declared a state of emergency. Nationalist leader Jomo Kenyatta (pictured opposite) believed complicit, was arrested. The killing of a white family in 1953 provoked Europeans to form their own militias.

In 1955, Baring offered an amnesty, but the offer was withdrawn after two white schoolboys were murdered. Some 70,000 suspects were imprisoned, and 10,000 officially killed by British forces to January 1956—full details of human rights abuses are only now emerging. In 1959, Baring suspended the state of emergency, but nationalist leaders boycotted negotiations until Kenyatta, now 71, could participate. In May 1963, he won the first multiracial election, declaring independence and an amnesty.

Suez Crisis

France had built a canal linking the Mediterranean and the Persian Gulf that opened in 1869, and Britain maintained it after gaining custody of Egypt, until a coup in 1952. New leader Colonel Nasser planned to nationalize the canal, using the revenue to fund assaults on Israel; he also courted the USSR.

Israeli general Moshe Dayan led incursions into Egypt—Nasser's inevitable reaction was used to legally justify an Anglo-French punitive expedition. Angry opposition in Britain contrasted this with recent acquiescence to the Soviet invasion of Hungary. British leader Anthony Eden, ill and heavily medicated, also misjudged international reaction. US President Eisenhower, a wartime general and colleague of France's President de Gaulle, refused to countenance the incursion; Soviet Premier Khrushchev threatened nuclear strikes (despite, we now know, lacking the ability), and initially successful action against Egypt was halted; France and the UK were forced to adjust to post-imperial *realpolitik,* but Nasser nevertheless abandoned his plan.

The Space Race

The potential for rocket flight beyond the atmosphere, fostered by Robert Goddard in the USA and hobbyists in Britain and the Soviet Union, was developed in Nazi Germany for military use. Postwar, the new Cold War rivals recruited Hitler's experts to work on both space travel and long-range missiles, and on October 4, 1957, the Soviets launched the first satellite, Sputnik I. Aside from the propaganda, America feared other payloads, and after Yuri Gagarin orbited Earth on April 12, 1961, President Kennedy vowed to land a man on the Moon by 1970. Neil Armstrong took the first step onto another world on July 20, 1969. Thereafter, interest in manned expeditions waned: Nixon, beleaguered by Vietnam, curtailed funding and the US space agency NASA concentrated on a reusable shuttle to near-Earth space, and unmanned probes to other planets. Weather, communications, and surveillance satellites make space economically significant, though in the West, private enterprise is now leading the way. Russia continues manned launches, while China and India are in a new space race.

Civil Rights

After Reconstruction gave way to Gilded Age "Jim Crow" laws (permitting segregation based on race), the fight for rights in the USA resumed. As a historical term, the US "Civil Rights Movement" denotes the period between the Supreme Court's 1954 *Brown v. Board of Education* decision (declaring school segregation impermissible) and the 1968 assassination of Martin Luther King, Jr (opposite).

King came to prominence with the Bus Boycott in Montgomery, Alabama (after activist Rosa Parks refused to give up her seat as legally required), preaching Christian nonviolence and using lawsuits, sit-ins, and marches. Equally influential was Malcolm X (assassinated in 1965). He initially advocated black nationalism, arguing that self-defense was justifiable in a country where the Ku Klux Klan murdered civil rights leaders and children (notoriously bombing a Birmingham, Alabama, church in 1963). The 1964 Civil Rights Act and the 1965 Voting Rights Act would end much explicitly legal, if not social, discrimination by 1968.

Cuba

The aftermath of the Spanish-American War left Cuba ostensibly independent, but in the US shadow; the 1901 Platt Amendment forced it to accept intervention, and US troops were frequently sent, implementing racial codes. Sugar became a major crop, and US interests came to control Cuba. Sergeant Fulgencio Batista led a revolt that put him in power from 1933.

Fidel Castro attempted several revolutions in the 1950s, finally succeeding in 1959 and enacting a socialist (soon one-party) state. Rich Cubans fled to Florida, while the US imposed sanctions that persist today (the USA also retains a naval base at Guantánamo Bay). A Kennedy-supported 1961 invasion at the Bay of Pigs was a fiasco, and after Cuba entered friendly but cautious relations with the USSR, Soviet Premier Khrushchev shipped nuclear missiles to the island (as America had to Britain and Turkey). Kennedy threatened nuclear war unless the ships turned around, and Khrushchev eventually capitulated. Castro ruled until 2008, succeeded by his brother Raul.

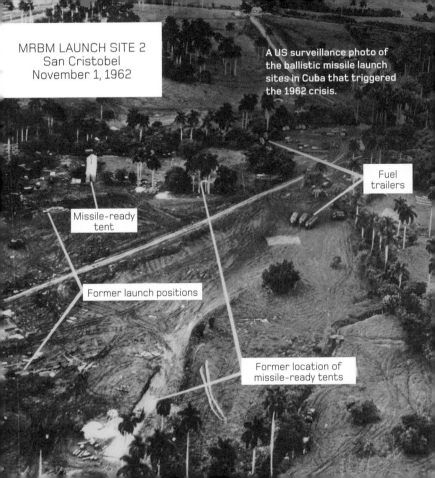

MRBM LAUNCH SITE 2
San Cristobel
November 1, 1962

A US surveillance photo of the ballistic missile launch sites in Cuba that triggered the 1962 crisis.

Fuel trailers

Missile-ready tent

Former launch positions

Former location of missile-ready tents

Environmentalism

The Agrarian Revolution and Chemistry had fed millions but destabilized complex natural cycles. Rachel Carson's 1962 book *Silent Spring*, describing the uncontrolled use of chemical pesticides, sparked public outrage and action. When Apollo 8 sent back the first pictures of the whole Earth from space over Christmas 1968, it underlined the fragility of the planet. The US government belatedly created an Environmental Protection Agency in 1970. Green parties sprang up, fighting causes from nuclear waste to genetically modified crops. In Europe, these have had small but significant electoral representation.

Industrial chemicals known as CFCs damaged the ozone layer that absorbs excessive ultraviolet sunlight. The 1987 Montreal Protocol agreed to an international ban, partly because the economic consequences were trivial. Scientists agree burning of fossil fuels is directly linked to global warming, threatening catastrophic consequences for civilization, but such warnings have so far largely been met with indifference and inaction.

"Winds of Change"

On January 6, 1960, Harold Macmillan (opposite) became the first British prime minister to visit sub-Saharan Africa, beginning his tour in newly independent Ghana. He had become leader after Suez, and feared a repeat of Partition as African nations became autonomous. Macmillan outlined the "wind of change" sweeping the continent, and the opportunities open to independent African nations if they avoided isolationism or favoring the USSR. On February 3 he gave the same speech in Cape Town, with dramatic results: South Africa's Verwoerd, seeing an attack on his racial policies, accelerated Apartheid, while Rhodesia's Ian Smith became increasingly isolationist (he was voted out in 1980 after Britain supervised transition in what is now Zimbabwe). Within three years Somalia, Nigeria, Sierra Leone, Tanzania, and Kenya were independent. France, meanwhile, cut its century-long ties with Algeria, abandoning its Harki loyalists and triggering a generation of terror attacks: the perceived French error here influenced both British policy in Ulster and later US persistence in Iraq.

Kennedy

Like Eisenhower before him, John F. Kennedy was a World War II hero who became president. Aided by his service record and a confident performance in televized debates, the dashing and charismatic "JFK" was elected in 1960. Kennedy and his wife Jacqueline associated with movie stars and astronauts, raising a young family in a celebrity White House (nicknamed "Camelot"). Much of his international policy was preoccupied with Cold War bickering; the Berlin Wall was erected in 1961, intervention in Cuba was a public failure, and the Vietnam conflict escalated. More positively, he founded the Peace Corps, bolstered the space program, and signed the Nuclear Test Ban Treaty with the USSR in 1963. Domestically, he initiated civil rights laws.

His assassination on November 22, 1963 shocked the world and sparked numerous conspiracy theories. His sucessor Lyndon Johnson skillfully deployed his legacy to push liberal legislation covering civil rights, the arts, and the "Great Society." The Kennedys would contribute many other figures to US politics.

Apartheid

The Union of South Africa formed in 1910, enacting laws that required black men to carry passes at all times, while barring them from voting or owning land. The National Party came to power in 1948, and its policy of apartheid took racial segregation beyond anything hitherto attempted: a category of "colored" was invented, arbitrarily denying rights to many more individuals on the grounds of mixed racial heritage.

At first, the African National Congress advocated passive resistance, but after a 1960 massacre of peaceful protestors at Sharpeville, they adopted violent tactics. ANC leader Nelson Mandela (1918–2013) was imprisoned in 1963. South Africa was ejected from the Commonwealth in 1961, but economic sanctions were few until the 1980s, by which time the country was a pariah. A state of emergency was declared in 1985 amid increasing black resistance. In 1990, President de Klerk began dismantling apartheid—Mandela was released and became, in 1994, the first black president in the first free election.

Vietnam War

Keen to restore American prestige after Cuba, President Kennedy incautiously increased the number of US troops in Vietnam. Lyndon Johnson made it a full-scale war, reducing his popularity at home. Television showed the war in full color; conscription was violently opposed; and the My Lai massacre, in which US soldiers killed and tortured hundreds of civilians, horrified mainstream America. Johnson's planned reforms, the "Great Society," collapsed, although civil rights advanced. Richard Nixon, elected in 1968 as fighting intensified, pursued an increasingly unwinnable war. Secretary of State Henry Kissinger promoted a "Domino Theory" that any state turning communist might "infect" its neighbors, justifying the bombing of unaligned Cambodia. "Peace with honor" meant no withdrawal until America had proved some (unspecified) point. However, as the electoral scandal of Watergate unfolded, Nixon abruptly announced an end to hostilities and fresh initiatives with the USSR and China. Saigon fell to the communists in 1975 and Vietnam was unified the following year.

Cultural Revolution

Mao's economic plan for China, the Great Leap Forward, ended in disaster, and other party leaders now jockeyed for position. During the 1950s, limited debate was tolerated, but in September 1965 Mao's ally Lin Piao urged a return to core values and demolition of hierarchies. Teachers, scholars, and engineers were forced to work manually on farms. Attacks on elitism, counter to millennia of Confucian customs, spread into ethnic violence. The Red Guard youth movement patrolled communities, identifying elitism and coordinating "local action" (mobs). At its peak, around 1968, the violence included assaults on foreigners and attacks on embassies (the Boxer Rebellion was cited approvingly). At least 1.5 million people died, and a generation missed even basic education.

Mao's initial aim was to outflank party leader Lui Shao-Chi (deposed in 1968). He now declared himself Supreme Leader, but after his death in 1976, his wife and her associates, the "Gang of Four," were arrested. The program came to an end in 1977.

Bangladesh

After Partition, two nations called "Pakistan" were created. Government was concentrated in West Pakistan, while East Pakistan, almost comparable to the old Bengal sultanate, had a majority of the population, but little power. Bengali language and culture were repressed, as were Hindu minorities.

The breakaway Aswana League won the 1970 election, but President Yahya Khan refused to recognize the result. His administration had failed East Pakistan in the Bhola Cyclone disaster and was increasingly isolated and unpopular. He now launched Operation Searchlight, an attempted genocide and purge of intellectuals, from which millions fled to India. The cyclone and later floods had awoken global sympathy, with rock star George Harrison launching the first benefit concert and world opinion hardening against Khan. India's welcoming of refugees was interpreted by Khan as an act of hostility, leading him to launch a short, disastrous war and abandon his Bengal massacres. East Pakistan became Bangladesh in 1971, with Aswana leader Sheikh Mujibur Rahman as its leader.

Idi Amin

U ganda was a nation created by British colonial fiat; in the 19th century, four distinct kingdoms and assorted tribes lived in its present-day footprint; empire introduced thousands of workers from India. In 1962, Milton Obote was elected first leader of independent Uganda, but internal disputes mounted. Eventually, he and his military protégé Idi Amin suspended the constitution and abolished the kingdoms.

When Obote visited Singapore in 1971, Amin seized a chance to overthrow him (Britain, more concerned by Obote's economic plans, underestimated a man who proclaimed himself Lord of all Beasts of the Earth and Fish of the Sea). In 1972, Amin expelled all 60,000 Ugandan Asians (many of whome settled in Britain), and gave their property to the army. Hundreds of thousands were massacred, but a 1978 declaration of war on Tanzania backfired and saw him forced into exile in Libya. Obote's return to power prompted civil war—rebel leader Yoweri Museveni became leader in 1986, restoring the kingdoms in 1993.

Allende and Chile

Chile had hitherto been held up as an example of democratic progress, but in 1970 had elected anti-Soviet socialist Salvador Allende. His novel remedies for soaring inflation and unemployment appalled US President Nixon, and the CIA were ordered to undermine Allende. After spending $7 million on propaganda and "Project FUBELT," they had fostered conditions for a military junta, led by General Augusto Pinochet, to seize power on September 11, 1973. At the time, with Nixon occupied by impeachment hearings and Vice President Agnew under arrest, Secretary of State Kissinger was *de facto* leader.

The precise US involvement in Allende's alleged suicide and Nobel prizewinning poet Pablo Neruda's suddenly fatal illness may never be known. Allende's economic and infomatic policies had almost stabilized the economy; Pinochet worsened it. The new regime was brutal; thousands were tortured, assassinated, or simply vanished. America never again intervened so blatantly, or with so little international censure.

Yom Kippur War

October 6, 1973 was a new moon, coinciding with Jewish Yom Kippur, Islamic Ramadan, and low tides. It was also a Saturday, the Jewish Sabbath; so when Egyptian forces forded the Suez Canal, recapturing territory won by Israel in 1967's Six Day War, no Israeli radio or television was broadcasting, and mobilization of defenses, including soldiers on leave for the holy week, was delayed. Meanwhile, Syria sent tanks into the Golan Heights. Egypt's President Sadat restored national pride but also sought to reinvigorate peace talks; Syria's Assad was out for victory. Israel's key weapon was its airforce, but Egypt had Soviet missiles capable of stopping them. Jets were more use against Syria, whose tanks paused for reinforcements some way from Jerusalem, buying time for Israel's US allies to rearm them. A ceasefire came on October 24, but Arab nations, appalled at US intervention, made use of their oil-production hegemony, and OPEC (the Organization of Petroleum Exporting Countries) quadrupled its prices in 90 days. Runaway inflation crippled Europe, and America went into recession.

Pol Pot

Cambodia's erratic ruler Prince Sihanouk spurned US aid and stayed out of the Vietnam War. With rice being sold over the border for high prices, he sent troops to supervise harvests and liquidate suspect peasants. A coup in 1970 provoked massacres of Vietnamese civilians in the country. A US–South Vietnamese force arrived, motivating indigenous communists. By 1973 this "Khmer Rouge" controlled all of Cambodia that could be governed. Kissinger ordered the country bombed, but this only hardened its resolve.

Saloth Sar, a French-educated admirer of both Mao and the Enlightenment, adopted the name "Pol Pot" and combined the "Great Leap Forward" and Cultural Revolution with the Terror: 1975 became Year Zero. The cities were emptied, with everyone forced to work the land; millions died through mismanaged collective farming, while arbitrary massacres continued and worsened. The Vietnamese invasion that began over Christmas 1978 was, to many, a form of salvation.

Ayatollahs in Iran

The term "ayatollah" refers to leaders of the Twelver Shi'ite Muslims, most prominently the rulers of modern Iran. Ayatollah Ruhollah Khomeini became Supreme Leader in 1979 after decades exiled in Paris. Persia became Iran in 1925 as Reza Shah, emulating Kemel Atatürk, attempted to secularize a nation that had been Shi'a since the Safavids. The Allies invaded in World War II (to secure oil and a supply route to Russia), forcing his abdication in favor of his son Mohammad Reza Pahlavi, who later recognized the new state of Israel.

In 1971, Iran celebrated 2,500 years of continuous monarchy in extravagant style, but Western support faded as it took a lead in OPEC after the Yom Kippur War. Clerics formed a nexus for discontent; popular uprisings resumed. The Shah extended an amnesty to opponents in exile, but in January 1979 went abroad himself to seek medical treatment. Prime Minister Shapour Bakhtiar invited Khomeini to return as a religious leader, but unleashed a full-scale Islamic revolution.

Bosnia

Following the collapse of the Soviet Union, ethnic and cultural rivalries in its satellite countries were unfrozen after years of communist repression. The zealotry that had triggered World War I in Sarajevo resumed after a 75-year hiatus.

Yugoslavia, a Treaty of Versailles construct of several different Slavic nationalities, had been held together for a generation by Josip Tito. His death in 1980 left the state slowly unraveling; Slovenia and Croatia broke away in 1991, while Bosnia-Herzegovina did the same in 1992. This region was roughly half Christian (Serbs and Croats) and half Muslim (Bosniacs); the Croats and Bosniacs had sought independence, while the Serbs wanted unification with Serbia. As war broke out, the Serbs began "ethnic cleansing," a genocidal effort to rid the region of Muslims. NATO sent troops in 1995, halting the conflict, but 100,000 died, and many more were made refugees. Hopes for a peaceful multiethnic state were lost in chaos, though many of the offenders were later brought to trial in international court.

The "War on Terror"

At the end of the Iran-Iraq War in 1988, Saddam Hussein used banned chemical weapons against Halabja, a Kurdish village near the Turkish border. But it took an invasion of oil-producing Kuwait in 1990 for the UK and US governments to turn against him; the UN narrowly sanctioned the military intervention of "Operation Desert Storm"—Iraq was defeated but Saddam was allowed to remain in power.

However, after Shi'ite terror-group Al Qaida attacked New York in 2001, President George W. Bush (whose father had been president in 1990) launched a war to depose Saddam. The official *casus belli* was the 1988 gassing and conjectured existence of Weapons of Mass Destruction (WMDs). Only the UK materially assisted in "Desert Shield." Saddam was tried and hanged by new Iraqi authorities, but no WMDs were found.

Bush Jr. made a spurious link between Al Qaida and Saddam, proclaiming US actions part of a "War on Terror." The Taliban, an Afghan Shi'ite sect supported by America in their resistance to the 1979 Soviet invasion, were the first target of this assault: NATO forces were deployed in Afghanistan, sustaining heavy casualties—neighboring Pakistan became a refuge for Taliban and Al Qaida members (notably Osama Bin Laden, the former US ally and Al Qaida founder), but was not invaded. Similarly, Iraq's neighbor and US ally Turkey was supported rather than condemned for increasing repression. Some European Muslims became radicalized, with Madrid and London among their targets; others became fearful as governments used security to justify increased surveillance and restrictions. Russia also used the perception of Islamic terror when attempting to stem Chechnya's bid for independence. A Russian-born Muslim's bomb attack on the Boston Marathon in 2013 consolidated a sense in the United State of global politics becoming local.

Since Bin Laden's death in 2011, movements such as Boko Haram, ISIS, and the Muslim Brotherhood have become notorious. Many governments use fear as a pretext for draconian laws but, in the face of the younger, more Westward-looking citizens' use of the internet, this has led to further tension and unlikely alliances between prodemocracy movements and hardline Shi'ite factions (as in the abortive Arab Spring of 2011).

The Credit Crunch

Since 1979, governments had experimented with deregulating financial services, and an automated international stock market began in 1986. China and the Middle East created a savings glut by lowering global interest rates and, in 2001, the head of the Federal Reserve reduced US rates to 1 percent. Investors looking for returns switched to buying mortgages, while in order to keep mortgage demand flowing, America lowered the amount of security required by the federal lenders.

Pension funds and European banks borrowed vast amounts of "cheap" American money to invest in mortgages, assuming that defaults would be localized. Instead, they snowballed as small investors lost income from earlier defaults, and a flood of repossessions devalued house prices. The federal lenders folded in August 2008, bankrupting the Lehman Brothers bank. The implosion triggered a global recession comparable to the Great Depression. Governments, forced into direct intervention, have since bailed out banks to salvage jobs and personal savings.

This graph based on UK statistics shows
the sudden plunge in economic output
and spike in interest rates that typified
the credit crunch in many countries.

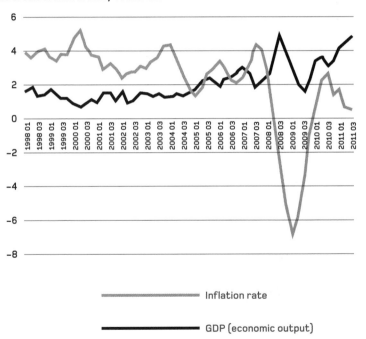

The Internet

The concepts of computing were developed in the 1930s, as data storage in binary "1" or "0" form suggested ways of performing abstract logical processes by mechanical or electronic means. During World War II, mathematician Alan Turing laid the framework for Colossus, a programmable machine used for deciphering Nazi signals—its existence was classified, but US researchers built similar devices soon after. William Shockley developed the semiconducting transistor in 1947, allowing the miniaturization of solid-state switches.

During the 1960s, the US military and universities worldwide developed ARPANET (an early computer network, including email) as British engineers established the packet-shifting system for relaying digital information in bursts. Tim Berners-Lee linked hypertext to earlier computer-sharing protocols in 1991, and the World Wide Web came into existence. Microsoft and America Online helped popularize it in the 90s, while ever cheaper, faster hardware domesticated interlinked computers.

Index

Quercus

New York • London

Text © 2015 2015 by Tat Wood and Dorothy Ail
First published in the United States by
Quercus in 2015

ISBN 978-1-62365-485-6

Library of Congress Control Number:
2014948267

Distributed in the United States and Canada by
Hachette Book Group
237 Park Avenue
New York, NY 10017

Manufactured in China
10 9 8 7 6 5 4 3 2 1
www.quercus.com